Economic Issues, Problems and Perspectives

T0295515

www.novapublishers.com

Economic Issues, Problems and Perspectives

Economic Crises: A Review and Directions for Research
Tulus T.H. Tambunan, PhD (Editor) – Professor, Economic Science, Universitas
Trisakti, Jakarta, Indonesia
Budi Santosa, PhD (Editor)
2022. ISBN: 978-1-68507-613-9 (Hardcover)
2022. ISBN: 978-1-68507-692-4 (eBook)

Advances in Capital Structure Research
Karel Marleau (Editor)
2021. ISBN: 978-1-53619-948-2 (Softcover)
2021. ISBN: 978-1-53619-969-7 (eBook)

Human Capital and Development
Gary I. Lilienthal (Editor)
2021. ISBN: 978-1-53619-714-3 (Hardcover)
2021. ISBN: 978-1-53619-733-4 (eBook)

The Impact of the COVID-19 Pandemic on International Oil Markets
Alexander G. Tvalchrelidze (Author)
2021. ISBN: 978-1-53619-595-8 (Hardcover)
2021. ISBN: 978-1-53619-698-6 (eBook)

Global Challenges of Digital Transformation of Markets
Elena de la Poza, PhD. (Editor)
Sergey E. Barykin, PhD. (Editor)
2021. ISBN: 978-1-53619-754-9 (Hardcover)
2021. ISBN: 978-1-53619-864-5 (eBook)

More information about this series can be found at
https://novapublishers.com/product-category/series/economic-issues-problems-
and-perspectives/

Raufhon Salahodjaev
Editor

Economic Growth and Wellbeing

Evidence from the Belt and Road Initiative Countries

www.novapublishers.com

NOTICE TO THE READER

Library of Congress Cataloging-in-Publication Data

ISBN: 978-1-68507-990-1

Published by Nova Science Publishers, Inc. † New York

Contents

Preface

Over the past two decades, there has been growing interest in understanding the drivers of rapid growth rates of countries in Central, East and South Asia. For example, countries such as China, Lao PDR, Vietnam, Uzbekistan and Mongolia were in the list of most rapid growing countries in the period of 2000-2020. As a result, these countries have considerably increased quality of life, standards of living and life satisfaction. For example, Uzbekistan is consistently ranked among one of the happiest developing countries in the world.

The present book attempts to build up on existing empirical research to offer all-encompassing evidence on some of the drivers and correlates of economic growth and quality of life in the Belt and Road Initiative countries. We explore the relationships between renewable energy and CO_2 emissions, financial development and economic growth, institutional and life satisfaction, among others.

While writing this book, we have used data from various sources, such as the World Bank, U.N., World Happiness Report and others. In addition, we have used various conventional theories and econometric estimations methods (Ordinary Least Squares, two-step Generalized method of moments, cointegration and others) to explore abovementioned relationships. This book further highlights that renewable energy, financial development, quality of institutions and human capital are instrumental for long-run economic growth and wellbeing of nations.

Raufhon Salahodjaev
Sharipov Kongratbay

Chapter 1

Tourism and Economic Growth

Sharipov Kongratbay[*]
Tashkent State University of Economics, Uzbekistan

Abstract

The aim of this chapter is to assess the relationship between tourism and economic growth in a sample of Belt and Road Initiative countries over the period of 2000-2019, using two-step GMM estimator. We rely on this approach to account for the problem of endogeneity and simultaneity. The empirical results suggest that tourism has positive impact on economic growth even after we account for potential drivers of economic growth. In particular, 1 percentage point increase in the size of tourism receipts as relative to GDP leads to 0.15 percentage points growth in GDP. The results of this study further confirm that tourism is a crucial driver of economic progress in BRI countries.

Keywords: tourism, economic growth, development

Introduction

Extant studies show that tourism is an important economic sector in less developed countries. It has been shown to be linked to sustainable development (Murphy and Price, 2005), income redistribution (Incera &

---

[*] Corresponding Author's Email: rector@tsue.uz.

In: Economic Growth and Wellbeing
Editor: Raufhon Salahodjaev
ISBN: 978-1-68507-990-1

Fernandez, 2015), and employment (Vanhove, 1981). Out of empirical research concerning the effects of tourism, one particular strand of studies has emerged that explores the relationship between tourism and economic growth. Sinclair (1998) published one of the earliest surveys of research on the tourism and economic progress based on studies that rely on single and system equation modeling tools. The author argues that empirical analysis of the importance of tourism for economic development is influenced by the multidimensional nature of the tourism industry. For example, the transportation sector, accommodation sector, quality of infrastructure and environmental quality are important drivers of tourism demand. Pablo-Romero and Molina (2013) conducted a review of published empirical evidence on the relationship between tourism and economic growth based on a sample of 87 papers. The authors of these papers have based their analysis on the nature of the data: time series, panel or cross-section. From these studies, 55 report that tourism has a causal effect on economic growth while 16 papers find bi-directional causality. The authors also determine that the scope of the effect of tourism on a nation's GDP differs not only across countries but also within one country. Gwenhure and Odhiambo (2017) conduct a review of empirical research on the direction of causal effects between tourism and economic growth for various groups of countries. The authors overall offer plenty of evidence, depending on the sample and empirical method, that tourism may have effect on GDP growth or tourism can be driven by economic development. The authors also reported that several studies fail to identify the causality between tourism and economic growth for Turkey, Brazil, Greece and Latin America. A more recent study, (Nunkoo et al., 2020), contributed to the debate on tourism and economic growth by offering the findings from a meta-regression analysis based on a collection of 113 published papers on tourism-growth nexus. The authors highlight "the presence of publication bias in the literature on this topic, where the majority of studies report positive and statistically significant estimates" (p. 404). The authors suggest that future studies should rely on different methodologies and empirical model specifications to assess the relationship between tourism and economic growth.

The contribution of this study is in two areas. First, this study focuses on the Belt and Road region a highly dynamic group of countries in the area of tourism sector. Some countries in this region have experienced significant growth in tourism industry. For example, in Uzbekistan according to the World Bank the number of international tourist arrivals increased 22-fold over the period 2000-2020[1]. Therefore, it is essential to assess the contribution of tourism sector to GDP growth. Second, we use two-step GMM estimator which allows us to resolve the problems of endogeneity and omitted variable bias that persists in cross-national research.

Review of Related Literature

A number of studies have explored the relationship between tourism and economics in the context of large N-samples. For example, Sequeira and Maçãs Nunes (2008) compare the effect of tourism on economic growth both in poor countries and globally across 90 countries, using data from the period of 1980-2002. The results of the GMM estimation suggest that tourism is an important driver of economic growth irrespective of the level of economic development or the sample size. Ivanov and Webster (2013) used a sample of 174 countries over the period of 2000-2010 and apply growth decomposition in order to explore the links between tourism and economic growth. Overall, the results from country by country analysis suggest that the effect of tourism on GDP is stronger in countries with a larger tourism sector relative to the size of the economy.

Brida et al., (2020) explored the link between tourism sector development and economic growth in a sample of 80 countries over the period of 1995-2016. The authors developed Minimal Spanning Tree and Hierarchical Tree to group nations based on performance. The authors reported findings that were contradictory to conventional tourism-led growth hypothesis research. The results imply that there is cluster performance among countries rejecting the conventional wisdom of a long-run economic development towards equilibrium.

Another group of studies assessed the non-linear relationship between tourism and economic growth. Po and Huang (2008) was one of the first studies to use a large sample of countries (n=88) over the period of 1995-2005 in order to document that there is a non-linear link between tourism receipts and GDP growth. The authors used threshold regression analysis and additionally controlled for services share to GDP and forested area.

Brida et al., (2016) examined non-linearity using M-Tar model for Brazil and Argentina for the years 1990-2011. The authors detect non-linear relationship only in the case of Brazil. Phiri (2016) explore linear and non-

---

[1] https://data.worldbank.org/indicator/ST.INT.ARVL?view=chart.

linear relationship between tourism proxies and economic growth in South Africa for the period 1995-2014. Using Enders and Granger cointegration approach, the authors found that tourism is causal to economic growth in linear specification, while there is bi-directional causality between tourism and economic growth in non-linear framework. Moreover, the authors also stress that tourism receipts have greater importance to economic growth compared to the number of arrivals. The same results are found in Muhtaseb and Daoud (2017) for Jordan over the period of 1998-2015, using Engel Granger cointegration model. The linear model confirms tourism led growth hypothesis, while the non-linear model reports bi-directional causality between tourism and economic growth. In a different study, Karimi (2018) relies on NARDL method to assess the non-linear relationship between tourism and economic growth in Malaysia for the years 2001-2015. The results from asymmetric models suggest that tourism has an overall positive effect on GDP growth in the long run and there is no relationship on growth in the short run.

The tourism-growth nexus has been carefully examined in the context of geographical regions. For example, Roudi et al., (2019) applied the ARDL cointegration approach and Granger causality test to assess the effect of tourism on economic growth in small island developing states over the period of 1995-2014. The authors highlight that the share of tourism earnings in exports is relatively high and an overdependence on the tourism sector may affect sustainable development. The results suggest that there is bi-directional causality between tourism and GDP growth and unidirectional between tourism and energy use. Therefore, the authors conclude that tourism should increase economic progress in the region and, at the same time, tourism may lead to higher energy demand. Mohapatra (2018) models the effect of tourism receipts on GDP growth in South Asian Association for Regional Cooperation (SAARC) countries over the period of 1995-2014. The results from Granger causality tests and panel FMOLS show that tourism receipts have causal effect on economic growth. Olabisi (2018) assessed the tourism-growth nexus in the sample of ECOWAS nations over the period 2007-2015 using a fixed effects regression estimator. The study found that various proxies of tourism are not significantly linked to GDP. Only human capital and investment rate are positive antecedents of economic growth. The study suggests that focuing on hard infrastructure would help to promote economic growth. Hakan et al., (2015) explored the relationship between tourism and economic growth in a sample of next 11 nations for the years 1995-2013. This study highlights that it is important to assess the next 11 sample as it has not been explored in the context of tourism-growth nexus. The authors used panel cointegration (FMOLS and DOLS) estimators. The empirical results suggest that there is unidirectional causality from tourism to GDP: 1% increase in tourism receipts arrivals leads to 0.06-0.08% increase in GDP. For example, Fayissa et al., (2008) investigated the relationship between tourism and economic growth for a sample of 42 African nations for the years 1995-2004. The authors, using fixed-effects, random-effects and GMM estimator overall document that tourism receipts have a positive impact on GDP per capita. Nene and Taivan (2017) used cointegration tests, vector error correction model and Granger causality test to explore the tourism-growth nexus across 10 Sub-Saharan Africa (SSA) countries over the period 1994 to 2014. Economic growth drives tourism development in 4 SSA countries, while tourism has a causal effect on economic growth in 6 SSA countries. The authors suggest that policymakers in countries where tourism development is influenced by economic need to allocate greater resources to the tourism industry in order to bolster tourism as one of the determinants of economic progress.

Antonakakis et al., (2015) assessed the relationship between tourism and economic growth by applying novel spillover index method for 10 European countries for the years 1995-2012. The results from Granger causality tests suggest that the direction of causality and the magnitude of the effect between tourism and GDP growth differ across countries and context, such as in the case of the Great Recession or the Eurozone debt crisis. The authors also discover that during macroeconomic turbulence years, economic growth drove the tourism sector. The authors concluded that countries within Europe suffering from a fiscal crisis should adopt policy measures that simulate different type of tourism such as cultural, religious or conference tourism. Selimi et al., (2017) assessed the impact of tourism on economic growth in six Western Balkan countries over the years from 1988 to 2014. The econometric results based on fixed effects and the Hausman Taylor IV estimator suggest that tourism has positive impact on GDP per capita. However, one of the limitations of the study is that it does not rule out the problem of endogeneity and small sample size. Motsa et al., (2021) focused on the role of regional tourism on regional economic growth in Europe over the period 2015 to 2019. The correlational analysis suggests that domestic tourism is an important predictor of regional GDP growth rates in 5 countries: Bulgaria, Germany, Greece, Spain and Italy. At the same time, it is negatively correlated with GDP growth rates in the countries of Belgium, Czech Republic and Estonia.

Lee and Brahmasrene (2013) explored the links between tourism, economic growth, FDI and CO_2 emissions in European Union for the years

1988-2009. The results from the panel cointegration method suggest that there is a long-run relationship between countries within the EU. Tourism and FDI have a positive impact on economic growth, while tourism reduces CO2 emissions. In a similar vein, Balsalobre-Lorente and Leitão (2020) used different methods such as panel fully modified least squares (FMOLS), panel dynamic least squares (DOLS) and fixed effects (FE) to explore the relationship between tourism, trade, economic growth, carbon emissions and renewable energy in 28 EU member states over the period 1995 to 2014. The study found that tourism, trade and green energy foster economic growth, while economic growth is also positively related to carbon emissions.

Proença and Soukiazis (2008) applied the Barro and Sala-i-Martin convergence model for Southern European countries (Spain, Portugal, Italy and Greece) over the period 1990-2004. The results suggest that tourism not only increases the quality of economic conditions in this region but also speeds up economic convergence. More recently, Haller et al., (2021) applied the convergence model on the larger sample of 28 European countries over the period 2012 to 2018. The results somewhat differ from Proença and Soukiazis (2008). While tourism has a positive impact on GDP growth, the role of tourism in economic convergence was very weak. The study concluded that economic convergence in EU does not significantly depend on tourism sector development.

Wu and Wu (2019) also applied the Granger causality test to the causality between tourism and economic growth in 11 Asian countries over the period 1995 to 2015. Tourism causes economic growth in Cambodia, China and Malaysia. In contrast, the data for Hong-Kong, Indonesia and Philippines show that tourism is driven by economic development. A bi-directional causality between tourism and economic growth was discovered for Macau and Singapore.

Narayan et al., (2010) investigated the importance of the tourism sector in promoting the economic growth of Pacific Island countries for the years 1988-2004. The study used cointegration and Granger causality test to examine this relationship. Tourism has a significant positive influence on economic growth in this region. Moreover, the effect is strongest in Papua New Guinea. However, the study also highlights that the tourism sector brings with it a number of challenges. First, the tourism in this country depends on imports of food due to underdeveloped agriculture sector. Apart from that, political stability and environmental quality are important factors that can promote the long-term development of tourism sector. Tugcu (2014) focuses on a sample of nations that border the Mediterranean Sea. In a similar vein, the author uses cointegration and Granger causality tests for the years 1998-2011. The findings show that the effects depend on variables within each country and the specifics of their tourism sector development. For example, feedback hypothesis is confirmed for European countries and neutrality hypothesis is confirmed for African nations. Therefore, European countries gain greater economic benefits from the development of tourism sector.

It is also important to note that a number of studies conjecture that the relationship between tourism and GDP growth is influenced by other economic variables. For example, Sokhanvar (2019) finds that FDI may play an important role in tourism-growth nexus for European countries. Using impulse response function, the authors show that FDI is negatively related to GDP growth, and insignificantly linked to the tourism sector. In the case of Poland, their tourism sector has no effect on GDP while for Bulgaria and Spain tourism promotes economic growth. Yazdi et al., (2017) also explored the relationship between tourism, FDI and economic growth in case of Iran over the period 1985-2013. The results from ARDL and VECM show that tourism has positive impact on economic growth both in the short and long run. The Granger causality test also displays bi-directional causality between tourism and economic growth. Meivitawanli (2018) also explored the relationship between tourism, economic growth and FDI in a sample of 18 OECD countries over the period 2005-2012 with the aid of a GMM estimator. The findings show that an FDI driven tourism sector is not significantly related to economic growth. Moreover, human capital and trade openness are not linked to FDI in tourism. Yu-Chi and Lin (2018) used the Granger causality test and cointegration method to explore the relationship between FDI, tourism and GDP growth in Taiwan over the period 1976 to 2016. While these variables have a long run relationship, there is bidirectional causality between GDP and tourism arrivals.

Apart from FDI, several other studies have explored the relationship between tourism, trade and FDI. For example, Suresh et al., (2018) focused on India over the period 1993 to 2014 using the Granger causality test and frequency-domain causality. The empirical results show that tourism and GDP have bidirectional causality, and that trade openness and tourism also have bidirectional causality. Jebli et al., (2019) assessed the dynamic links between tourism, trade, FDI, GDP growth and CO_2 emissions in Central and South American countries over the period of 1995-2010 using Granger causality tests, FMOLS and DOLS. The results suggest that tourism decreases environmental degradation, as well as increases FDI and trade openness. Economic growth has a causal effect on tourism. Therefore, the study fails to confirm TLGH for this sample. Akadiri and Akadiri (2021) explored the causal links between tourism, exchange rate and economic growth in Island states for the years 1995-2016. The results from panel bootstrap cointegration tests suggest that tourism promotes economic growth, while exchange rates have a significant influence on the tourism sector. Moreover, exchange rate also has a causal impact on GDP growth. El Menyari (2021) explores the relationship between FDI, tourism and GDP growth in Morocco over the years 1983-2018. The results from ARDL and Granger causality tests show that tourism-oriented FDI decreases GDP growth. FDI and tourism arrivals have positive causal effect on economic growth. The Granger causality test shows unidirectional causality from tourism to GDP growth.

Kumar et al., (2019) considers the relationship between ICT, tourism and economic growth in Israel over the period of 1960-2016. Using ARDL modeling, the results suggest that ICT and tourism are causal to economic growth, and ICT also has a causal effect on tourism. Ohlan (2017) use the Bayer and Hanck combined test, ARDL and VECM to explore the relationship between tourism, financial development and economic growth in India over the period 1960 to 2014. The estimates show that these variables are cointegrated and that tourism increases economic growth both in the short and long-run. The role of human capital is considered in a study by Fahimi et al., (2018) for micro-states for the years 1995-2015. The authors used the Granger causality test in their empirical analysis. The study shows that tourism increases economic growth and improves human capital. Moreover, human capital also has a positive impact on GDP growth. Therefore, tourism seems to have both direct and indirect effects on GDP growth in micro-states. Zhang and Zhang (2021) used a VECM estimator to assess the relationship between tourism, economic growth, energy and CO_2 emissions in China for the years 2000-2017. First, there is a long-run relationship between these variables. Second, there is bi-directional causality between tourism and economic growth in China. In addition, energy consumption has unidirectional causality to tourism, CO_2 emissions and GDP growth. Shi et al., (2020) empirically models the relationship between energy, tourism, GDP and CO_2 emissions for a large sample of countries. The panel cointegration results show that tourism arrivals lead to a rise in CO_2 emissions. Shaheen et al., (2019) explored the relationship between tourism, energy, CO_2 and economic growth in top 10 touristic countries for the period 1995 to 2016. The study shows that GDP per capita is non-linearly related to CO_2 emissions. Economic growth has a causal effect on tourism income and CO_2 emissions determine tourism departures. The study also highlights the importance of promoting eco-tourism to mitigate the effects of climate change. Tsaurai (2018) augments the tourism-growth debate for South African countries with the financial development variable. The author, using OLS, fixed and random effects models, found that both the financial and touristic sectors have a positive influence on economic growth. Moreover, the study shows that tourism and financial development are complementary factors for economic progress. The relationship between energy, tourism and economic growth has also been explored by Sghaier et al., (2019) for the countries of Tunisia, Egypt and Morocco for the years 1980-2014. The study examines short and long-term relationships using the ARDL method. The study indicated that tourism degrades environmental quality in Egypt and improves it in Morocco.

The role of globalization in the tourism-growth relationship has been studied by Salifou and Haq (2017) in the context of 11 ECOWAS nations (Benin, Burkina Faso, Ivory Coast, Ghana, Guinea, Guinea-Bissau, Mali, Niger, Nigeria, Senegal and Togo) over the period of 1990-2010. The results from FMOLS and DOLS regressions show that tourism and globalization have a significant positive impact on GDP growth. Rivera (2017) explored the relationship between human capital, tourism and GDP growth in Ecuador using VECM and Granger causality tests. The study finds that: (1) tourism is driven by human capital development; (2) there is bidirectional causality between human capital and economic growth; and (3) economic growth is causal to tourism sector development. Therefore, the study concludes that tourism does not promote economic growth or human capital in Ecuador. Işik (2017) relies on Emirmahmutoglu–Kose bootstrap Granger non-causality test to explore the relationship between tourism, energy and economic growth in a sample of the 10 most visited nations. The results suggest that the directions of causality are at best mixed and depend on other country's specific aspects.

Kreishan (2010) used cointegration and Granger causality tests to explore the effect of tourism on economic growth in Jordan over the period of 1970-2009. Jordan is considered one of the countries with fastest growing tourism market. Thus, it is essential to assess its influence on GDP. The empirical findings suggest that there is long run unidirectional causality from tourism to GDP growth. Therefore, including the tourism sector in long-term development plans is essential for policymakers. Gautam (2011) confirmed the positive effect of tourism on the economic growth of Nepal, using data for Nepal for the period 1974 to 2009. Moreover, the results from the Granger causality test and cointegration method show that there is bi-directional causality between these two variables. Another study by Suresh and Senthilnathan (2014) focused on Sri Lanka, using data from 1977-2012, applying also the cointegration method and Granger causality test. However, the results significantly differ compared to Nepal: economic growth is causal to tourism earnings in Sri Lanka. The study highlights that it is important to adopt policies that will stimulate the growth of the tourism sector so that it can drive economic development. Jaforullah (2015) tested whether tourism promotes economic growth in New Zealand for the years 1972-2012. The study, relying on cointegration tests and VECM, found that tourism is causal to economic growth and the coefficient of elasticity is 0.4. The study highlights that the policymakers in New Zealand should continue promoting tourism competitiveness in order to boost economic growth. Akan et al., (2007) explored the role of tourism in economic growth in Turkey from the years 1985 to 2007 using VAR, cointegration and the Granger causality test. The empirical findings suggest international tourism arrivals have a positive impact on the economic growth of Turkey. In addition, the study finds that there is a long-run multiplier effect of tourism sector development. Jin (2011) relied on the VAR model to explore the relationship between tourism and GDP growth in Hong Kong for the years 1974-2004. The author includes tourism arrivals in the Cobb-Douglas production function in the theoretical framework. The author highlights that Hong Kong may serve as an interesting case as 50% of total arrivals are tourists, 25% are businessman and 25% are transit travelers or occasional visitors. The results suggest that tourism has pro-growth effects only in the short run, while in the long run tourism is not a driver of economic growth. Kibara et al., (2012) revisited the tourism-growth nexus for Kenya over the period 1983 to 2010, using ARDL bounds testing. Kenya has significant potential for the tourism sector development as the country is "endowed with unique tourist attractions consisting of tropical beaches, diverse wildlife in natural habitats, scenic landforms, archaeological sites, and a rich indigenous cultural heritage which combine to form a unique tourist product" (p. 518). Indeed, the results of the study show that tourism has causal effect on economic growth in both the short and long run. Bouzahzah and El Menyari (2013) further explored the tourism-growth relationship in Africa, focusing on Morocco and Tunisia over the period of 1980-2010. The results from VECM, Granger causality test and cointegration suggest that tourism is causal to economic growth only in the short run. However, in the long run economic growth drives tourism sector development. In turn, Akinboade and Braimoh (2010) focused on South Africa for the years 1980 to 2005. The authors applied the VAR and Granger causality test in their empirical analysis. The findings show that there is a unidirectional causal effect of tourism on economic growth both in the short run and in the long run.

Kadir and Karim (2012) relied on panel cointegration analysis and the Granger causality test to assess the effect of tourism arrivals from 5 ASEAN countries on economic growth in Malaysia over the period 1998 to 2005. The empirical findings suggest that causality runs from tourism to economic growth in the short and long run. Therefore, the authors recommend to further boost investments in the tourism infrastructure in order to attract more international tourists. Surugiu and Surugiu (2013) assess the relationship between tourism and economic growth in Romania from 1988 to 2009. The results based on VECM and Granger causality test suggest that a tourism-led growth hypothesis is valid for Romania.

Data and Methods

The dependent variable in this study is GDP growth from World Bank. Figure 1 plots the average levels of GDP growth over the period 2000-2019. These values range from 0.1% in Yemen to 9.6% in Myanmar.

We use two proxies for tourism: tourism receipts as % of GDP and tourism receipts per capita. The data come from World Bank. Figure 2 plots the average values of tourism receipts relative to GDP over the period 2000-2015. For example, the data shows that tourism accounts for 61.3% of GDP in Maldives.

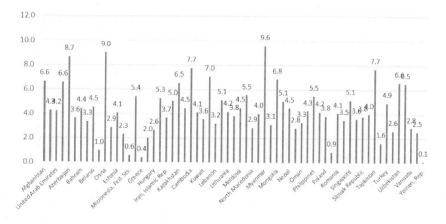

Figure 1. GDP growth, 2000-2019.

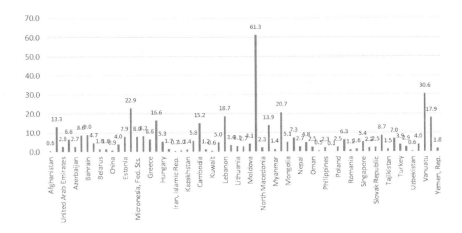

Figure 2. Tourism receipts as % of GDP, 2000-2015.

Table 1. Descriptive statistics

Variable	Mean	Std. Dev.	Min	Max
GDP growth, %	4.29	4.64	-33.10	54.16
GDP per capita, constant international dollars	19138.42	17847.01	1093.79	102494.90
Tourism receipts per capita	533.88	833.65	0.09	6461.85
Tourism receipts as % of GDP	6.77	9.66	0.01	81.09
Gross fixed capital formation as % of GDP	23.94	6.39	2.92	57.71
Trade as % of GDP	101.17	55.91	0.17	437.33
General final government consumption as % of GDP	15.56	4.78	3.46	30.00
Renewable energy as total energy production	21.62	22.99	0.00	91.31
FDI as % of GDP	5.96	21.38	-41.51	451.64
GDP deflator	6.93	10.97	-26.10	185.29

In order to assess the relationship between tourism and economic growth we estimate the following regression model:

$$Growth = a_0 + a_1 Tourism + \gamma X + \varepsilon \qquad (1)$$

where *Growth* is GDP growth, *Tourism* is one of the proxies for the size of the tourism sector, X is a vector of control variables and ε is an error term. Following empirical studies on economic growth, we include GDP per capita, investment rate, trade openness, government size, renewable energy, FDI and

GDP deflator as our control variables (Keho, 2017; Pegkas, 2015). The data comes from World Bank. We include GDP per capita in our model to account for the effect of economic convergence across countries. We estimate Eq. (1) using a two-step GMM estimator. The descriptive statistics are reported in Table 1.

Results

The main empirical results are reported in Table 2. Column 1 presents the results for tourism receipts per capita. The estimate is positive and significant, suggesting that tourism has a positive impact on GDP growth. For example,

Table 2. Main results

	I	II
Growth$_{t-1}$	0.3014	0.3255
	(8.76)***	(10.36)***
GDP per capita$_{t-1}$	-4.0139	-2.6408
	(6.10)***	(4.14)***
Tourism per capita	0.0019	
	(5.46)***	
Tourism as % GDP		0.1454
		(3.68)***
Investment	0.1499	0.1794
	(5.86)***	(5.50)***
Trade openness	0.0115	0.0263
	(1.28)	(3.24)***
Government size	-0.2133	-0.3039
	(1.96)*	(2.85)***
Renewable energy	-0.1581	-0.1485
	(4.61)***	(4.30)***
FDI	-0.0061	-0.0064
	(2.74)***	(3.43)***
Inflation	0.0082	0.0058
	(0.40)	(0.29)
Constant	37.6524	23.8341
	(6.19)***	(3.59)***
Hansen p-value	0.088	0.113
N	794	794

* $p < 0.1$; ** $p < 0.05$; *** $p < 0.01$.

1 standard deviation increase in tourism receipts per capita leads to 1.6 percentage points increase in GDP growth rate. Turning to control variables, we find that GDP growth is faster in countries with higher investment rates. Greater government size inhibits economic growth (Chen and Lee, 2005). On the other hand, we also find that FDI and renewable energy is negatively related to GDP growth in BRI countries. Column 2 further confirms that tourism receipts as % of GDP also exert positive impact on GDP growth. For example, 1 percentage point increase in tourism receipts leads to 0.15 percentage points increase in GDP growth. Overall, the results confirm that tourism is an important driver of GDP growth in BRI countries.

Conclusion

The aim of this chapter is to assess the relationship between tourism and economic growth in a sample of Belt and Road Initiative countries over the period of 2000-2019, using two-step GMM estimator. We rely on this approach to account for the problem of endogeneity and simultaneity. The empirical results suggest that tourism has positive impact on economic growth even after we account for potential drivers of economic growth. In particular, 1 percentage point increase in the size of tourism receipts as % of GDP leads to 0.15 percentage points growth in GDP. The results of this study further confirm that tourism is crucial driver of economic progress in BRI countries.

Our study has a number of policy implications. First, BRI countries that aim to increase economic growth via offering employment opportunities should adopt policies aimed at the development of the tourism sector. Tourism sectors have spillover effects on services, transportation and retail. Second, the development of tourism sectors may be promoted by offering fiscal incentives for entrepreneurs to set up companies in the tourism industry. Apart from that, the government may use grants and low interest loans to attract entrepreneurs in the industry. Another important factor to consider is the commitment of BRI countries to curb CO_2 emissions and reduce carbon footprint. Therefore, agritourism and sustainable tourism may be important types of tourism for sustainable development.

This study has a number of limitations that should be addressed by future studies. Due to the lack of international data, we do not consider that role that COVID19 pandemic played in affecting economic growth and tourism sector internationally. Therefore, the effect of tourism on GDP growth may differ in the post-pandemic era. Apart from that the use of two-step GMM estimator does not permit us to explore the bi-variate causality between tourism and GDP, if it exists in our data. This has been left as avenue for future research. Prospective studies can extend our results in a number of ways. First, it is important to explore the relationship between tourism and economic growth using sub-national data. Second, it would be interesting to assess whether tourism may have effects on CO_2 emissions and other environmental outcomes.

References

Akadiri, S. S., & Akadiri, A. C. (2021). Examining the causal relationship between tourism, exchange rate, and economic growth in tourism island states: evidence from second-generation panel. *International Journal of Hospitality & Tourism Administration*, *22*(3), 235-250.

Akan, Y., Arslan, İ., & Isik, C. (2007). The impact of tourism on economic growth: The case of Turkey. *Journal of Tourism*, *9*(1), 1-24.

Akinboade, O. A., & Braimoh, L. A. (2010). International tourism and economic development in South Africa: A Granger causality test. *International Journal of Tourism Research*, *12*(2), 149-163.

Antonakakis, N., Dragouni, M., & Filis, G. (2015). How strong is the linkage between tourism and economic growth in Europe?. *Economic Modelling*, *44*, 142-155.

Balsalobre-Lorente, D., & Leitão, N. C. (2020). The role of tourism, trade, renewable energy use and carbon dioxide emissions on economic growth: evidence of tourism-led growth hypothesis in EU-28. *Environmental Science and Pollution Research*, *27*(36), 45883-45896.

Bouzahzah, M., & El Menyari, Y. (2013). International tourism and economic growth: the case of Morocco and Tunisia. *The Journal of North African Studies*, *18*(4), 592-607.

Brida, J. G., Lanzilotta, B., & Pizzolon, F. (2016). Dynamic relationship between tourism and economic growth in MERCOSUR countries: A nonlinear approach based on asymmetric time series models. *Economics Bulletin*, *36*(2), 879-894.

Brida, J. G., Gómez, D. M., & Segarra, V. (2020). On the empirical relationship between tourism and economic growth. *Tourism Management*, *81*, 104131.

Chen, S. T., & Lee, C. C. (2005). Government size and economic growth in Taiwan: A threshold regression approach. *Journal of Policy modeling*, *27*(9), 1051-1066.

El Menyari, Y. (2021). Effect of tourism FDI and international tourism to the economic growth in Morocco: Evidence from ARDL bound testing approach. *Journal of Policy Research in Tourism, Leisure and Events*, *13*(2), 222-242.

Fahimi, A., Saint Akadiri, S., Seraj, M., & Akadiri, A. C. (2018). Testing the role of tourism and human capital development in economic growth. A panel causality study of micro states. *Tourism management perspectives*, *28*, 62-70.

Fayissa, B., Nsiah, C., & Tadasse, B. (2008). Impact of tourism on economic growth and development in Africa. *Tourism Economics*, *14*(4), 807-818.

Gautam, B. P. (2011). Tourism and economic growth in Nepal. *NRB Economic Review*, *23*(2), 18-30.

Gwenhure, Y., & Odhiambo, N. M. (2017). Tourism and economic growth: A review of international literature. *Tourism: An International Interdisciplinary Journal*, *65*(1), 33-44.

Hakan, K. U. M., Aslan, A., & Gungor, M. (2015). Tourism and economic growth: the case of next 11 countries. *International Journal of Economics and Financial Issues*, *5*(4), 1075-1081.

Haller, A. P., Butnaru, G. I., Hârşan, G. D. T., & Ştefănică, M. (2021). The relationship between tourism and economic growth in the EU-28. Is there a tendency towards convergence?. *Economic Research-Ekonomska Istraživanja*, *34*(1), 1121-1145.

Incera, A. C., & Fernández, M. F. (2015). Tourism and income distribution: Evidence from a developed regional economy. *Tourism Management*, *48*, 11-20.

Işik, C., Doğan, E., & Ongan, S. (2017). Analyzing the tourism–energy–growth nexus for the top 10 most-visited countries. *Economies*, *5*(4), 40.

Ivanov, S. H., & Webster, C. (2013). Tourism's contribution to economic growth: a global analysis for the first decade of the millennium. *Tourism Economics*, *19*(3), 477-508.

Jaforullah, M. (2015). International tourism and economic growth in New Zealand. *Tourism Analysis*, *20*(4), 413-418.

Jebli, M. B., Youssef, S. B., & Apergis, N. (2019). The dynamic linkage between renewable energy, tourism, CO 2 emissions, economic growth, foreign direct investment, and trade. *Latin American Economic Review*, *28*(1), 1-19.

Jin, J. C. (2011). The effects of tourism on economic growth in Hong Kong. *Cornell Hospitality Quarterly*, *52*(3), 333-340.

Kadir, N., & Karim, M. Z. A. (2012). Tourism and economic growth in Malaysia: Evidence from tourist arrivals from ASEAN-S countries. *Economic research-Ekonomska istraživanja*, *25*(4), 1089-1100.

Karimi, M. S. (2018). The linkage between tourism development and economic growth in Malaysia: a nonlinear approach. *International Economic Journal*, *32*(1), 53-65.

Keho, Y. (2017). The impact of trade openness on economic growth: The case of Cote d'Ivoire. *Cogent Economics & Finance*, *5*(1), 1332820.

Kibara, O. N., Odhiambo, N. M., & Njuguna, J. M. (2012). Tourism and economic growth in Kenya: An empirical investigation. *International Business & Economics Research Journal (IBER)*, *11*(5), 517-528.

Kreishan, F. M. (2010). Tourism and economic growth: The case of Jordan. *European Journal of Social Sciences*, *15*(2), 63-68.

Kumar, R. R., Stauvermann, P. J., Kumar, N., & Shahzad, S. J. H. (2019). Exploring the effect of ICT and tourism on economic growth: a study of Israel. *Economic Change and Restructuring*, *52*(3), 221-254.

Lee, J. W., & Brahmasrene, T. (2013). Investigating the influence of tourism on economic growth and carbon emissions: Evidence from panel analysis of the European Union. *Tourism management*, *38*, 69-76.

Meivitawanli, B. (2018). Foreign Direct Investment in Tourism and Economic Growth: Panel Data of OECD Countries. *International Journal of Advanced Engineering Research and Science*, *5*(9).

Muhtaseb, B. M., & Daoud, H. E. (2017). Tourism and economic growth in Jordan: Evidence from linear and nonlinear frameworks. *International Journal of Economics and Financial Issues*, 7(1), 214-223.

Murphy, P. E., & Price, G. G. (2005). Tourism and sustainable development. *Global tourism*, 3, 167-193.

Narayan, P. K., Narayan, S., Prasad, A., & Prasad, B. C. (2010). Tourism and economic growth: a panel data analysis for Pacific Island countries. *Tourism economics*, 16(1), 169-183.

Nene, G., & Taivan, A. (2017). Causality between tourism and economic growth: Evidence from Sub Saharan Africa (SSA). *The Journal of Developing Areas*, 51(2), 155-169.

Nunkoo, R., Seetanah, B., Jaffur, Z. R. K., Moraghen, P. G. W., & Sannassee, R. V. (2020). Tourism and economic growth: A meta-regression analysis. *Journal of Travel Research*, 59(3), 404-423.

Ohlan, R. (2017). The relationship between tourism, financial development and economic growth in India. *Future Business Journal*, 3(1), 9-22.

Olabisi, E. O. (2018). Revisiting the tourism-economic growth nexus: the case of economic community of West African States. *Izvestiya. Journal of Varna University of Economics*, 62(1), 21-30.

Pablo-Romero, M. D. P., & Molina, J. A. (2013). Tourism and economic growth: A review of empirical literature. *Tourism Management Perspectives*, 8, 28-41.

Pegkas, P. (2015). The impact of FDI on economic growth in Eurozone countries. *The Journal of Economic Asymmetries*, 12(2), 124-132.

Phiri, A. (2016). Tourism and Economic Growth in South Africa: Evidence from Linear and Nonlinear Cointegration Frameworks. *International Research Journal*, 14(1), 31-53.

Po, W. C., & Huang, B. N. (2008). Tourism development and economic growth–a nonlinear approach. *Physica A: Statistical mechanics and its applications*, 387(22), 5535-5542.

Proença, S., & Soukiazis, E. (2008). Tourism as an economic growth factor: a case study for Southern European countries. *Tourism Economics*, 14(4), 791-806.

Rivera, M. A. (2017). The synergies between human development, economic growth, and tourism within a developing country: An empirical model for Ecuador. *Journal of destination marketing & management*, 6(3), 221-232.

Roudi, S., Arasli, H., & Akadiri, S. S. (2019). New insights into an old issue–examining the influence of tourism on economic growth: evidence from selected small island developing states. *Current Issues in Tourism*, 22(11), 1280-1300.

Salifou, C. K., & Haq, I. U. (2017). Tourism, globalization and economic growth: A panel cointegration analysis for selected West African States. *Current Issues in Tourism*, 20(6), 664-667.

Shaheen, K., Zaman, K., Batool, R., Khurshid, M. A., Aamir, A., Shoukry, A. M., ... & Gani, S. (2019). Dynamic linkages between tourism, energy, environment, and economic growth: evidence from top 10 tourism-induced countries. *Environmental Science and Pollution Research*, 26(30), 31273-31283.

Sghaier, A., Guizani, A., Jabeur, S. B., & Nurunnabi, M. (2019). Tourism development, energy consumption and environmental quality in Tunisia, Egypt and Morocco: A trivariate analysis. *GeoJournal*, 84(3), 593-609.

Selimi, P., Sadiku, D. L., & Sadiku, P. (2017). The Impact of Tourism on Economic Growth in the Western Balkan Countries: An Empirical Analysis. *International Journal of Business and Economic Sciences Applied Research (IJBESAR)*, *10*(2), 19-25.

Sequeira, T. N., & Maçãs Nunes, P. (2008). Does tourism influence economic growth? A dynamic panel data approach. *Applied economics*, *40*(18), 2431-2441.

Shi, H., Li, X., Zhang, H., Liu, X., Li, T., & Zhong, Z. (2020). Global difference in the relationships between tourism, economic growth, CO2 emissions, and primary energy consumption. *Current Issues in Tourism*, *23*(9), 1122-1137.

Sinclair, M. T. (1998). Tourism and economic development: A survey. *The journal of development studies*, *34*(5), 1-51.

Sokhanvar, A. (2019). Does foreign direct investment accelerate tourism and economic growth within Europe?. *Tourism Management Perspectives*, *29*, 86-96.

Suresh, K. G., Tiwari, A. K., Uddin, G. S., & Ahmed, A. (2018). Tourism, trade, and economic growth in India: A frequency-domain analysis of causality. *Anatolia*, *29*(3), 319-325.

Suresh, J., & Senthilnathan, S. (2014). Relationship between tourism and economic growth in Sri Lanka. *Published as the 7th chapter of a book entitled "Economic Issues in Sri Lanka" compiled by Dr. S. Vijayakumar*, 115-132.

Surugiu, C., & Surugiu, M. R. (2013). Is the tourism sector supportive of economic growth? Empirical evidence on Romanian tourism. *Tourism Economics*, *19*(1), 115-132.

Tsaurai, K. (2018). The role of financial sector development in the tourism-growth nexus: A case of Southern African countries. *Journal of Economics and Behavioral Studies*, *10*(3), 100-110.

Tugcu, C. T. (2014). Tourism and economic growth nexus revisited: A panel causality analysis for the case of the Mediterranean Region. *Tourism management*, *42*, 207-212.

Vanhove, N. (1981). Tourism and employment. *International Journal of Tourism Management*, *2*(3), 162-175.

Wu, T. P., & Wu, H. C. (2019). Tourism and economic growth in Asia: A bootstrap multivariate panel Granger causality. *International Journal of Tourism Research*, *21*(1), 87-96.

Yazdi, S., Homa Salehi, K., & Soheilzad, M. (2017). The relationship between tourism, foreign direct investment and economic growth: evidence from Iran. *Current Issues in Tourism*, *20*(1), 15-26.

Zhang, J., & Zhang, Y. (2021). Tourism, economic growth, energy consumption, and CO2 emissions in China. *Tourism Economics*, *27*(5), 1060-1080.

Chapter 2

Financial Development, Trade Openness and Economic Growth

Eshov Mansur[*]

Tashkent State University of Economics, Tashkent, Uzbekistan

Abstract

The aim of this study is to explore the long-term relationship between financial development, trade and economic development in 43 Belt and Road economies over a period between 1995-2018. Our findings demonstrate a positive long-term association between trade and income per capita, as well as between financial development index and income per capita. Coefficients are significant at p < 0.01. Considering the historical background and geography of Belt and Road economies, trade still remains a significant growth factor. The effect of the financial development index is slightly greater, highlighting the relative importance of well-developed financial markets over the trade shares.

Keywords: financial development, trade, economic growth

Financial Development and Economic Growth

There is substantial research that assesses the finance-growth nexus. For example, Jung (2017) explores the relationship between FD and EG in South

[*] Corresponding Author's Email: m.eshov@tsue.uz.

In: Economic Growth and Wellbeing
Editor: Raufhon Salahodjaev
ISBN: 978-1-68507-990-1
© 2022 Nova Science Publishers, Inc.

Korea between 1961-2013. The results from the VAR empirical modeling suggest that variables are cointegrated. Moreover, the VECM and Granger causality show that financial development has a positive and causal effect on GDP growth. The authors highlight that the rapid economic success of South Korea is partly explained by the development of the financial sector.

Ono (2017) explores the link between financial development and economic growth in Russia prior to and after the global financial crisis. The study relies on the vector autoregression model and considers the role of the global energy sector and exchange rate. The results suggest that before and after the crisis, the causality ran from economic growth to the financial sector. Moreover, money supply has no significant impact on GDP growth, confirming demand-following response. In a different study, Škare et al., (2019), using data for Poland over the period 1990-2018, tests the effect of financial development on economic growth. Using vector autoregression model (VECM), the authors find that financial development positively impacts GDP growth and credit growth. However, the authors conclude that more empirical evidence is needed to robustly assess the finance-growth nexus in the case of Poland. Chen et al., (2020) investigate the asymmetric effect of the financial sector on GDP growth in Kenia using data for 1972-2017 and adopting non-linear auto-regressive distributive lag (NARDL) method. The findings show that positive shocks to financial development increase economic growth.

Moreover, the authors highlight the importance of a stable macroeconomic environment and effective government spending to promote economic growth. The authors conclude that "appropriate policies that favor low inflation and reduced government spending, expansion of feasibly reformed financial institutions, capital accumulation, and increased resource mobilization should be instituted if real growth is to positively happen" (p. 1).

Lenka and Sharma (2020) argue that the choice of variables may matter in exploring the relationship between financial development and economic growth. The study using data for India over the period 1980-2017 creates an FD index with the aid of principal component analysis. The results from ARDL and VECM methods suggest that FD positively impacts GDP growth in the short- and long-run, while there is also bi-directional causality between these two variables. Puatwoe and Piabuo (2017) assess the relationship between FD and EG in Cameroon for the period 1980-2014. The authors use financial depth and financial efficiency as proxies for the FD. The results from ARDL modeling suggest that FD has a positive impact on economic growth in the long run. Therefore, the study confirms the instrumental role of financial development in the economic growth of Cameroon. Sumarmi (2019) explores the effect of FD on EC in Indonesia for the period 2005-2016, using ARDL method. The empirical findings show that the variables are cointegration and in the long-run financial development has a positive impact on GDP growth rates.

Ibrahim and Alagidede (2018) explore the relationship between financial development and economic growth across 29 Sub-Sahara African countries over the period 1980-2014. The study uses system GMM estimator and finds that financial development has a positive impact on national output, but the estimate depends on the nature of the financial system. The authors highlight that a rapid rise in credit to GDP ratio may lead to more financial resources being allocated to risky and insecure projects that can lead to bankruptcy and overall inflation. In a more recent study, Opoku et al., (2019) focus on assessing the causal effect of financial development on economic growth across 47 African countries over the period 1980-2016, using a frequency-domain spectral causality estimator. The authors document the existence of the neutrality hypothesis, which implies that there is no significant effect of financial development on GDP growth in the region. Bandura and Dzingirai (2019) contribute to this debate by accounting for the effect of institutional quality. The authors rely on data for 27 Sub-Sahara African countries from 1982-2016. Using system GMM estimator, the study establishes a U-shaped relationship between financial development and GDP growth with the turning point of 33-37%. Moreover, the authors show that the impact of the financial sector on economic growth is stronger in countries with higher quality of institutions.

Guru and Yadav (2019) explore the relationship between financial development and GDP growth for BRICS over the period 1993-2014. The study relies on the stock market and banking sector size as proxies for financial development. Using system GMM estimator, the study finds that financial development has a positive effect on economic growth. Similarly, time stock market and banking sectors are complementary factors in economic growth. Swamy and Dharani (2018) assess the causal relationship between financial development and economic growth in a sample of 24 high-income countries over the period 1983-2013. The linear regression modeling suggests a negative effect in the long run. At the same time, the panel Granger causality test shows bi-directional causality between FD and EG. The authors also find that macroeconomic instability (inflation and high-interest rate) have negative interactive effects on the FD-EG nexus, while globalization has a positive impact.

Erdogan et al., (2020) explore the role of financial development in the context of natural resources and economic growth nexus. The study uses data for the next 11 countries (Bangladesh, Egypt, Indonesia, Iran Islamic Republic, South Korea, Mexico, Nigeria, Pakistan, the Philippines, Turkey, and Vietnam) for the years 1996-2016. Using panel threshold regression analysis, the authors document that once the level of financial development exceeds 45%, natural resources have positive impact on economic growth. Therefore, the study seems to support non-linearity in the links between the financial sector and GDP growth. In a similar vein, Tariq et al., (2020) investigate the non-linear relationship between financial development and GDP growth in Pakistan for the period 1980-2017. The study using quantile regression finds a U-shaped link between finance and GDP growth, suggesting "when financial development of Pakistan surpasses the threshold level, it contributes more towards economic growth" (p. 161). Therefore, the authors suggest that policymakers should adopt policies that boost financial development in Pakistan in the mid-term perspective.

Introduction

Do trade liberalization and financial development (FD) promote economic growth (EG) in BRI countries? This question has motivated numerous scholars to conduct empirical research to shed light on the relationship between trade openness (TO), financial development (FD), and economic growth. Some earlier studies have explored the links between trade openness and economic growth (Lutz & Singer, 1994; Sinha and Sinha, 1999). This study contributes to this debate by exploring the relationship between trade openness, financial development, and economic growth in BRI countries.

The level of trade openness has been steady across in the BRI countries. For example, the share of trade as % of GDP rose from 81.7% in 1990 to 107.9% in 2019. As a result, the level of trade openness in 2019 was significantly above that in other regions such as Sub-Saharan Africa, MENA or East Asia and Pacific. Moreover, the scatterplot between trade openness and GDP per capita for the BRI countries suggest a positive correlation. At the same time, existing data from the World Bank suggests that the average share of domestic credit to GDP increased from 32.9% in 1991 to 60.6% in 2019.

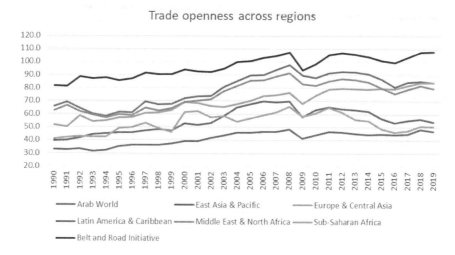

Figure 1. Trade openness across regions.

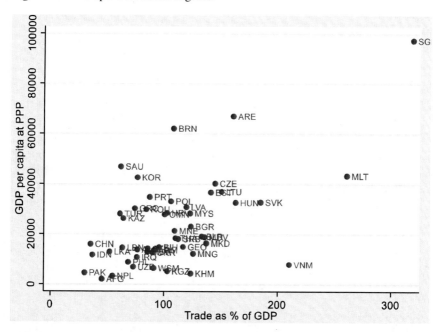

Figure 2. Scatterplot between TO and GDP per capita, 2019.

Considering the sharp increase in the levels of TO and FD, it is essential to explore their effects on GDP. The research on the BRI countries in this area largely focuses on the effects of TO and FD on environmental indicators (Sun et al., 2019; Saud et al., 2019) while overlooking the influence of these variables on GDP growth. Hence our study aims to close the existing gap in the empirical literature by exploring the long-term relationship between financial development, trade and economic development in 43 Belt and Road economies. Our analyses cover a period between 1995-2018.

Review of the Most Recent Empirical Evidence

Trade and Economic Growth

Rafindadi and Ozturk (2017) examine the interrelations between TO, EG, FD, and energy consumption in South Africa during 1970-2011. The study applies a wide range of methods such as ARDL, VECM, Granger causality and Ng-Perron tests to assess the causal links. The econometric results show that TO has effect on energy use which in turn is related to EG. In a similar vein, FD has a causal impact on energy consumption. Therefore, policymakers should liberalize the trade regime and financial sector in South Africa to promote long-run economic growth. In another study, Malefane and Odhiambo (2018), using data for South Africa over the period 1975-2014, explore the relationship between TO and EG. The results based on ARDL modeling show mixed results. Some of the trade proxies (total trade as a share of GDP) are positively related to EG, while others (exports as a share of GDP and imports as a share of GDP) are insignificantly linked to EG. Abdulkadhim (2020) assesses the relationship between TO and EC in UAE between 1980-2014. The study relies on dynamic OLS (DOLS) and Fully Modified OLS (FMOLS) to assess the short- and long-run relationship. The statistical results show that trade openness has a significant and robust positive impact on GDP growth. The study highlights the need to adopt export stimulating measures to promote economic growth rates.

Malefane and Odhiambo (2019) use ARDL to explore the effect of TO on EC in Lesotho from 1979-2013. The authors fail to identify the significant effect of trade liberalization on economic growth, using various proxies for trade openness in both the short and long run. The authors suggest that trade openness will influence GDP growth rate once a certain level of economic development in Lesotho is achieved.

Iyke (2017) used fixed effects regression estimator to test the relationship between TO and EG in a sample of 17 Central and Eastern European (CEE) countries over the period 1994-2014. The findings confirm the presence of the positive effect of trade liberalization on economic growth. Moreover, the results increase in size once Croatia and Estonia (two closed countries) are removed from the sample. Therefore, reforms that lead to an increase in exports are associated with an increase in GDP in these economies.

Nursini (2017) assess the mutual effects of fiscal policy and trade on EG in Indonesia for the years 1990-2015. The cointegration method results suggest that government spending on human capital and trade openness positively impacts EG. However, overall government spending decreases the GDP growth rates in both short- and long-run. In the case of China, the causality runs from economic growth to trade indicators, while there is no significant relationship between trade and GDP growth for Brazil and Russia. Burange et al., (2019) investigate the relationship between TO and EC for BRICS countries over the period 1981-2013. The VAR and cointegration methods produced mixed results.

Raghutla (2020) explores the relationship between TO and EG for a sample of 5 emerging markets from 1993-2016 using cointegration methods. The panel data results suggest that TO has a positive impact on GDP growth in the long run. Moreover, the causality tests give evidence that there is a unidirectional causality running from EG to TO. The study highlights that trade liberalization will increase income in emerging economies.

Keho (2017) explores the links between TO and EG in Cote d'Ivoire over the period 1965-2014, using ARDL and cointegration methods. The results show that TO positively impacts GDP growth in the short- and long-run. Moreover, investment rate and trade are complementary variables in fostering economic growth.

Silajdzic and Mehic (2018) explore the relationship between TO and EG in 10 Central-Eastern European countries over 1995-2013. The results from the fixed effects regression estimator show that an increase in the trade levels has a positive impact on economic growth. For example, a 10% increase in trade openness is associated with an 8% increase in GDP per capita growth rate.

Data and Methods

Our study explores long-term relationship between financial development, trade and economic development in 43 Belt and Road economies[1]. Our

---

[1] Albania, Armenia, Azerbaijan, Bahrain, Bangladesh, Belarus, Bhutan, Bosnia and Herzegovina, Brunei Darussalam, Bulgaria, Cambodia, China, Czech Republic, Egypt,

analyses cover a period between 1995-2018 and total number of observations is 1032. Economic development is measured as a following function:

$$Y_{i,t} = f(FD_{i,t}, T_{i,t}, K_{i,t}, D_{i,t}, Inf_{i,t}) \tag{1}$$

where Y is income per capita, FD is financial development index, T – trade, K - capital investment, D - democracy and Inf is inflation. i stands for the number of panels and t stands for the number of years. Table 1 provides variables description.

Dependent variable is economic development measured by GDP per capita. In our sample mean income per capita yields 9.1 thousand $US.

The main independent variables are trade and financial development index. Trade is measured as a sum of exports and imports over GDP. Average trade share in our sample is 95 percent of the GDP, which shows relative openness of Belt and Road economies compared to world's average of 60 percent.

Empirical literature usually proxies financial development by such variables as the share of credit to private sector broad money and stock market capitalization (Hassan et al., 2011; Anton & Afloarei Nucu, 2020; Isaeva et al., 2021). Although such indicators indeed provide some valuable insights on the financial system of the country, it considers its dimensions only and ignores its multidimensional nature. Our study thus employs a composite indicator of financial development developed by International Monetary Fund, covering more than 180 economies between 1980-2013. The index considers development of financial institutions (banks, insurance companies, mutual and pension funds) and financial markets (stock and bond markets). Index defines financial development by the size and liquidity of financial markets (depth), ability of individuals and companies to access financial services (access) and ability of institutions to provide financial services at low cost and with sustainable revenues, and the level of activity of capital markets (efficiency) (Svirydzenka, 2016). Financial development index is ranged between 0-1, where higher values correspond to better financial performance. In Belt and Road economies, financial market is relatively underdeveloped with financial development index yielding 0.33.

Estonia, Georgia, Greece, Hungary, India, Indonesia, Israel, Jordan, Kazakhstan, Kenya, Lebanon, Malaysia, Mongolia, Nepal, Oman, Pakistan, Philippines, Poland, Romania, Russian Federation, Saudi Arabia, Singapore, Slovak Republic, Slovenia, Sri Lanka, Thailand, Turkey, Ukraine, Vietnam.

Control variables include investment in fixed capital, democracy and inflation. Fixed capital investment is proxied by gross fixed capital formation and mean investment in our sample is 25% of GDP. Democracy is measured as an average of political rights and civil liberties ranged between 1-7 where lower values correspond to more democratic institutions. Average democracy score in our sample is around 4. Inflation is measured by GDP deflator, which is about 12% as Table 1 shows.

Table 1. Descriptive statistics

Variable	Indicator	Source	Mean	Std. Dev.
Y	GDP per capita (constant 2010 US$)	WDI	9145.73	10123.55
T	Trade (% of GDP)	WDI	94.74	56.56
FD	Financial development index	IMF	0.33	0.16
K	Gross fixed capital formation (% of GDP)	WDI	24.81	7.84
D	Average of political rights and civil liberties	Freedom house	3.90	1.77
Inf	GDP deflator (annual %)	WDI	11.75	45.00

Further, we rewrite the equation with some variables transformed into natural logarithms to improve their distributional properties:

$$\ln Y_{i,t} = \beta_0 + \beta_1 \ln T_{i,t} + \beta_2\, FD_{i,t} + \beta_3 K_{i,t} + \beta_4 D_{i,t} + \beta_5 \ln Inf_{i,t} \qquad (2)$$

where lnY stands for natural logarithm of income per capita, lnT- for natural logarithm of trade share, FD – for financial development index, K – for gross fixed capital formation as a share of GDP, D for democracy index, and Inf natural log of GDP deflator. Before logarithmic transformation of GDP deflator, we normalize the variable due to its negative values. Correlation coefficient between original and normalized indicator equals to one.

Before cointegration and causality analysis we investigate integration order by employing four panel unit-root tests - Im, Pesaran and Shin (2003) and Maddala and Wu (1999).

To explore cointegrating relationship, we employ panel cointegration test proposed by Pedroni (1999). To assure robustness of results, we additionally employ Kao and Westerlund panel cointegration tests (Kao, 1999; Westerlund, 2005). Pedroni's cointegration test tests the hypothesis of no-cointegration by employing parametric and non-parametric test statistics, which are further divided by group and panel statistics. The null hypothesis is rejected if the majority of statistics support the alternative one. After conducting cointegration test, we report long-term coefficients with Fully Modified Ordinary Least Squares (FMOLS).

Further, we check causal relationship between economic growth, by employing Dumitrescu and Hurlin's (2012) panel Granger causality test. The benchmark equation is as follows:

$$Y_{i,t} = \alpha_i + \sum_{k=1}^{K} \gamma_{ik} Y_{i,t-k} + \sum_{k=1}^{K} \beta_{ik} X_{i,t-k} + \varepsilon_{i,t} \tag{3}$$

where, in our case, Y is per capita income and X is either trade or financial development index. Noteworthy, all observations are stationary in a strongly balanced panel dataset for individual i in period t.

Table 2. Panel unit root test results

Form	Variable	Test		
		IPS	ADF Fisher	PP Fisher
Level	ln Y	7.9333	43.8932	72.2509
		(1.0000)	(1.0000)	(0.8551)
First-difference	Δ ln Y	-10.0531***	315.3538***	445.3649***
		(0.0000)	(0.0000)	(0.0000)
Level	ln T	-0.6575	136.8637***	88.3384
		(0.2554)	(0.0004)	(0.4100)
First-difference	Δ ln T	-15.1903***	511.4093***	819.1963***
		(0.0000)	(0.0000)	(0.0000)
Level	FD	0.1062	117.6329**	114.3941**
		(0.5423)	(0.0133)	(0.0220)
First-difference	Δ FD	-17.0033***	563.3021***	1073.1398***
		(0.0000)	(0.0000)	(0.0000)
Form	Variable	Test		
		IPS	ADF Fisher	PP Fisher
Level	K	-0.5105	198.5031	112.8312**
		(0.3048)	(0.0000)	(0.0278)
First-difference	Δ K	-13.4084***	380.7627***	629.6263***
		(0.0000)	(0.0000)	(0.0000)
Level	D	-1.7786**	201.8155***	249.3321***
		(0.0377)	(0.0000)	(0.0000)
First-difference	Δ D	-15.5437***	413.1635***	880.7098***
		(0.0000)	(0.0000)	(0.0000)
Level	ln Inf	-13.7273***	432.1109***	827.6443
		(0.0000)	(0.0000)	(0.0000)
First-difference	Δ ln Inf	-20.2278***	951.5792***	1935.7527***
		(0.0000)	(0.0000)	(0.0000)

Note: ***, ** and * indicate significance at 1%, 5% and 10% levels, respectively.

Dumitrescu and Hurlin's test check the hypothesis of non causal relationship by estimating Eq. 3 for each individual panel and then average the estimates to construct Wald statistics. Final testing is based on z-bar and z-tilde statistics: the latter is preferable for samples with relatively small number of observations (N) and time periods (T) (Lopez and Weber, 2017).

We first check if trade and financial development individually cause economic development. After this, we check the opposite: if economic development causally related to trade and financial development.

Empirical Results

We first report panel unit-root test results in Table 2. As we can see, democracy index and inflation are stationary both at level after first-differencing. On the other hand, income per capita is not stationary at level under three tests. Other variables provide more complex results, with some tests report stationarity at level and the rest claiming otherwise. However, after detrending, all variables are stationary. According to Pedroni (1999), cointegration may exist for a "set of variables that are individually integrated of order one, some linear combination of which can be described as stationary." This implies that we can proceed with cointegration analysis since we confirmed the integration order.

Table 3. Panel cointegration results

Test Statistic	Dependent variable
	Δ ln Y
V-stat	-3.67***
Panel rho-stat	2.239***
Panel PP-stat	-3.507***
Panel ADF-stat	1.789*
Group rho stat	4.603***
Group PP stat	-2.88***
Group ADF stat	4.583***
Kao's ADF	-9.5754***
Variance ratio	10.3851***

Note: ***, ** and * indicate significance at 1%, 5% and 10% levels, respectively; Pedroni's test is one-tailed and critical value for 1% is 1.28.

Table 3 reports the results of Pedroni's cointegration test, which estimated our model with all variables integrated of order one and stationary. Additionally, Table 3 provides results for Kao and Westerlund's cointegration test to verify Pedroni's results. Our findings demonstrate a strong cointegrating relationship between the variables in our model. Six out of seven Pedroni's statistics strongly reject the null hypothesis of non-cointegrating relationship ($p < 0.01$). At the same time, Kao's statistics confirm Pedroni's findings as well as Westerlund's variance ratio ($p < 0.01$).

Finally, we report long-term coefficient by re-estimating our model with Fully Modified Ordinary Least Squares regression (Table 4). Our findings demonstrate a positive long-term association between trade and income per capita, as well as between financial development index and income per capita. Coefficients are significant at $p < 0.01$. Considering the historical background and geography of Belt and Road economies, trade still remains a significant growth factor. The effect of the financial development index is slightly greater, highlighting the relative importance of well-developed financial markets over the trade shares. Capital investment and inflation are positively associated with economic development in the long-term. Moreover, as coefficient of democracy index is negative, we can state that relatively democratic institutions associated with greater economic well-being at $p < 0.1$.

Table 4. FMOLS regression results

Variables	Δ ln Y
Δ ln T	0.03***
	(7.18)
Δ FD	0.17***
	(9.56)
Δ K	0.01***
	(35.78)
Δ D	-0.01*
	(-1.46)
Δ ln Inflation	0.01***
	(9.04)

Note: ***, ** and * indicate significance at 1%, 5% and 10% levels, respectively.

Finally, we estimate Eq. 3 to investigate the causal relationship between the variables. We first check if trade causes economic development and vice versa. Table 5 shows that income per capita causes trade at $p < 0.01$. In other words, growing income per capital increases the share of trade in GDP structure within the development course. As for financial development, two-way causality is observed. Financial development index causes per capita income at $p < 0.05$. At the same time, per capita income causes financial development at $p < 0.05$. Greater financial development enhances economic growth and economic growth, in turn, enhances the development of the financial sector.

Table 5. Panel causality test

Null hypothesis	Statistic z-bar tilde	Optimal number of lags (AIC)	Lags tested
$\Delta \ln T$ doesn't Granger-cause $\Delta \ln Y$	-0.2965 (0.7668)	1	1-5
$\Delta \ln Y$ doesn't Granger-cause $\Delta \ln T$	4.6867*** (0.0000)	2	1-5
ΔFD doesn't Granger-cause $\Delta \ln Y$	2.0560** (0.0398)	1	1-5
$\Delta \ln Y$ doesn't Granger-cause ΔFD	2.4336** (0.0150)	1	1-5

Note: ***, ** and * indicate significance at 1%, 5% and 10% levels, respectively.

Conclusion

In this chapter, we assess the long-term relationship between financial development, trade and economic development in 43 Belt and Road economies between 1995-2018. Our findings demonstrate a positive long-term association between trade and income per capita, as well as between financial development index and income per capita. Coefficients are significant at $p < 0.01$. Considering the historical background and geography of Belt and Road economies, trade still remains a significant growth factor. The effect of the financial development index is slightly greater, highlighting the relative importance of well-developed financial markets over the trade shares.

These findings highlight that policymakers in BRI countries should promote the development of the financial sector and adopt export-oriented policies to stimulate economic growth. These measures may include greater level of financial inclusion to society and economic agents. Economic growth may increase only when the financial resources are available for companies and households across different regions within a country. Apart from that, it is important to increase financial literacy, as human capital and financial capital go hand in hand in less-developed countries. Finally, fostering innovative development would increase the demand for financial resources, which in turn will have an effect on GDP growth.

References

Abdulkadhim, H. H. (2020). Trade Openness and Economic Growth: A Lesson from United Arab Emirates. *The Scientific Journal of Cihan University-Sulaimaniya*, 4(2), 115-129.

Anton, S. G., & Afloarei Nucu, A. E. (2020). The effect of financial development on renewable energy consumption. A panel data approach. *Renewable Energy*, 147, 330-338. https://doi.org/10.1016/j.renene.2019.09.005.

Bandura, W. N., & Dzingirai, C. (2019). Financial development and economic growth in Sub-Saharan Africa: the role of institutions. *PSL Quarterly Review*, 72(291), 315.

Burange, L. G., Ranadive, R. R., & Karnik, N. N. (2019). Trade openness and economic growth nexus: A case study of BRICS. *Foreign Trade Review*, 54(1), 1-15.

Chen, H., Hongo, D. O., Ssali, M. W., Nyaranga, M. S., & Nderitu, C. W. (2020). The asymmetric influence of financial development on economic growth in Kenya: evidence from NARDL. *SAGE Open*, 10(1), 1-17, 2158244019894071.

Dumitrescu, E. I., & Hurlin, C. (2012). Testing for Granger non-causality in heterogeneous panels. *Economic Modelling*, 29(4), 1450-1460.

Erdoğan, S., Yıldırım, D. Ç., & Gedikli, A. (2020). Natural resource abundance, financial development and economic growth: an investigation on Next-11 countries. *Resources Policy*, 65, 101559.

Guru, B. K., & Yadav, I. S. (2019). Financial development and economic growth: panel evidence from BRICS. *Journal of Economics, Finance and Administrative Science*.

Hassan, M. K., Sanchez, B., & Yu, J. S. (2011). Financial development and economic growth: New evidence from panel data. *The Quarterly Review of Economics and Finance*, 51(1), 88-104. https://doi.org/10.1016/j.qref.2010.09.001.

Ibrahim, M., & Alagidede, P. (2018). Effect of financial development on economic growth in sub-Saharan Africa. *Journal of Policy Modeling*, 40(6), 1104-1125.

Im, K. S., Pesaran, M. H., & Shin, Y. (2003). Testing for unit roots in heterogeneous panels. *Journal of Econometrics*, 115(1), 53-74. https://doi.org/10.1016/S0304-4076(03)00092-7.

Isaeva, A., Salahodjaev, R., Khachaturov, A., & Tosheva, S. (2021). The Impact of Tourism and Financial Development on Energy Consumption and Carbon Dioxide Emission: Evidence from Post-communist Countries. *Journal of the Knowledge Economy*. https://doi.org/10.1007/s13132-021-00732-x.

Iyke, B. N. (2017). Does trade openness matter for economic growth in the CEE countries?. *Review of Economic Perspectives*, 17(1), 3-24.

Jung, S. M. (2017). Financial development and economic growth: Evidence from South Korea between 1961 and 2013. *International Journal of Management, Economics and Social Sciences (IJMESS)*, 6(2), 89-106.

Keho, Y. (2017). The impact of trade openness on economic growth: The case of Cote d'Ivoire. *Cogent Economics & Finance*, 5(1), 1332820.

Lenka, S. K., & Sharma, R. (2020). Re-examining the effect of financial development on economic growth in India: Does the measurement of financial development matter? *Journal of Asia-Pacific Business*, 21(2), 124-142.

Lutz, M., & Singer, H. W. (1994). The link between increased trade openness and the terms of trade: An empirical investigation. *World Development*, 22(11), 1697-1709.

Maddala, G. S., & Wu, S. (1999). A Comparative Study of Unit Root Tests with Panel Data and a New Simple Test. *Oxford Bulletin of Economics and Statistics*, 61(S1), 631-652. https://doi.org/10.1111/1468-0084.0610s1631.

Malefane, M. R., & Odhiambo, N. (2018). Impact of Trade Openness on Economic Growth: Empirical Evidence from South Africa. *Economia Internazionale/International Economics*, 71(4), 387-416.

Malefane, M. R., & Odhiambo, N. M. (2019). Trade openness and economic growth: empirical evidence from Lesotho. *Global Business Review*, 0972150919830812.

Nasir, H., Majeed, S., & Aleem, A. (2018). Does financial development leads economic growth? Evidence from emerging Asian markets. *Asian Economic and Financial Review*, 8(5), 599.

Nursini, N. (2017). Effect of fiscal policy and trade openness on economic growth in Indonesia: 1990-2015. *International Journal of Economics and Financial Issues*, 7(1).

Ono, S. (2017). Financial development and economic growth nexus in Russia. *Russian Journal of Economics*, 3(3), 321-332.

Opoku, E. E. O., Ibrahim, M., & Sare, Y. A. (2019). The causal relationship between financial development and economic growth in Africa. *International Review of Applied Economics*, 33(6), 789-812.

Pedroni, P. (1999). Critical Values for Cointegration Tests in Heterogeneous Panels with Multiple Regressors. *Oxford Bulletin of Economics and Statistics*, 61(S1), 653-670. https://doi.org/10.1111/1468-0084.0610s1653.

Rafindadi, A. A., & Ozturk, I. (2017). Dynamic effects of financial development, trade openness and economic growth on energy consumption: Evidence from South Africa. *International Journal of Energy Economics and Policy*, 7(3), 74-85.

Raghutla, C. (2020). The effect of trade openness on economic growth: Some empirical evidence from emerging market economies. *Journal of Public Affairs*, 20(3), e2081.

Saud, S., Chen, S., & Haseeb, A. (2019). Impact of financial development and economic growth on environmental quality: an empirical analysis from Belt and Road Initiative (BRI) countries. *Environmental Science and Pollution Research*, 26(3), 2253-2269.

Silajdzic, S., & Mehic, E. (2018). Trade openness and economic growth: Empirical evidence from transition economies. In *Trade and global market*. IntechOpen.

Sinha, T., & Sinha, D. (1999). The relation between openness and economic growth: postwar evidence from 124 countries. *Seoul Journal of Economics*, 12.

Škare, M., Sinković, D., & Porada-Rochoń, M. (2019). Financial development and economic growth in Poland 1990-2018. *Technological and Economic Development of Economy*, 25(2), 103-133.

Sumarni, L. (2019). Financial development and economic growth in Indonesia: An ARDL-Bounds testing approach. *Economic Journal of Emerging Markets*, 11(1), 89-96.

Eshov Mansur

Sun, H., Attuquaye Clottey, S., Geng, Y., Fang, K., & Clifford Kofi Amissah, J. (2019). Trade openness and carbon emissions: Evidence from belt and road countries. *Sustainability*, 11(9), 2682.

Svirydzenka, K. (2016). Introducing a New Broad-Based Index of Financial Development (SSRN Scholarly Paper ID 2754950). *Social Science Research Network*. https:// papers.ssrn.com/abstract=2754950.

Swamy, V., & Dharani, M. (2018). An alternate approach in exploring the causal link between financial development and economic growth - Evidence from advanced economies. *International Journal of Finance & Economics*, 23(1), 55-76.

Tariq, R., Khan, M. A., & Rahman, A. (2020). How does financial development impact economic growth in Pakistan?: New evidence from threshold model. *The Journal of Asian Finance, Economics, and Business*, 7(8), 161-173.

Chapter 3

Financial Development and Renewable Energy Consumption

Abdurakhmanova Gulnora[*]

Tashkent State University of Economics, Uzbekistan

Abstract

The current study explores the effect of financial development on renewable energy consumption in Europe and Central Asia during 1995-2015. Pedroni's cointegration test is employed to reveal the existence of long-term cointegrating relationship and ARDL-PMG re-estimate the equation to obtain short- and long-term coefficients. Empirical results reveal negative and significant relationship between financial development and renewable energy consumption in the short term and positive and significant relationship in the long term. In the short term, countries are growth-oriented and may be focused more on carbon-intensive sectors. In the longer run, however, climate issues and shortage of natural resources may facilitate the adoption of renewable energy sources.

Keywords: financial development, renewable energy consumption, cointegration

---

[*] Corresponding Author's Email: g.abdurakhmanova@tsue.uz.

In: Economic Growth and Wellbeing
Editor: Raufhon Salahodjaev
ISBN: 978-1-68507-990-1

Introduction

Energy crisis, depletion of natural resources and climate change issues have made adoption of renewable energy sources inevitable for future sustainable development. Driven by technological innovation and consequent cost reduction, the energy transition has already begun, yet green technologies still experience harsh competition with heavily subsidized fossil fuels in some countries. In 2017, only 17% of total energy consumption fell on renewables, with 789 million people worldwide lacking access to electric power[1]. This is especially relevant for resource-abundant countries, which are redundant to switch to renewables due to the high potential of carbon-intensive energy technologies. Scaled adoption of renewables requires energy policies to address both the subsidies and impacts of fossil fuels while facilitating more finance for renewable energy projects[2]. In this sense, a reliable financial system is crucial as it serves as an intermediary of financing and investing in renewable technologies.

The role of financial sector development in energy consumption is moderately studied (Janpolat et al., 2021; Islam et al., 2013; Shahbaz & Lean, 2012; Sadorsky, 2011, 2010). On the one hand, financial development may increase conventional energy consumption and harm the environment by facilitating financial flows to carbon-intensive sectors such as industry, mining, and transport (Abokyi et al., 2019; Gokmenoglu & Sadeghieh, 2019; Boutabba, 2014). At the same time, financial system improvement enhances innovation, research, and development. It also enables financial instruments for investing in clean energy (Salman & Atya, 2014), decreasing the share of conventional energy use.

The current study sheds light on the effect of financial development on renewable energy consumption in Europe and Central Asia between 1995 and 2015. We employ the panel cointegration approach introduced by Pedroni (1999) and obtain short- and long-term coefficients by estimating the equation using Autoregressive Distributed Lag Pooled Mean Group Estimator (ARDL-PMG) for panel data developed by Pesaran et al. (1999). The study extends the emerging literature on the financial development-renewables relationship, employing a composite measure of financial development calculated by the IMF.

[1] UN, 2021. https://unstats.un.org/sdgs/report/2020/goal-07/.
[2] UNEP, 2021. https://www.unep.org/explore-topics/energy/what-we-do/renewable-energy.

The remainder of the chapter is as follows: section 2 describes the link from the theoretical point of view, relying on previous studies; sections 3 and 4 provide data and methods descriptions, respectively; section 5 discusses the empirical results, and section 6 concludes the main findings.

Literature Review

Renewable Energy and Economic Growth

During the last 20 years, empirical literature expanded regarding studying the relationship between renewable energy and economic growth. Some studies report a positive association between the variables. For example, Lin & Moubarak (2014) observe a positive effect of renewable energy on economic growth in China despite a relatively low share in total energy consumption. Pao & Fu (2013) obtain similar findings for Brazil: renewable energy increased economic growth between 1980-2010. At the same time, for both China and Brazil, economic growth promotes renewable energy consumption. Similarly, Ntanos et al. (2018) report a positive relationship between renewable energy and economic growth in 25 European countries' economies between 2007-2016, again highlighting the role of income level: stronger association was observed in countries with relatively higher GDP. Haseeb et al. (2018) emphasize the importance of renewable energy consumption for economic wellbeing in Malaysia. Omri et al. (2015) explore the link in 17 developed and developing countries, confirming the positive association between nuclear and renewable energy and economic growth. Similar results were also obtained in black Sea and Balkan countries (Koçak & Şarkgüneşi, 2017), MENA countries (Kahia et al., 2017), South Asian countries (Rahman & Velayutham, 2020), emerging economies (Ozcan & Ozturk, 2019), and renewable energy-consuming countries (Shahbaz et al., 2020). On the other hand, some existing literature provides evidence on the adverse effect of renewable energy consumption on economic growth. For example, Ocal & Aslan (2013) observe a significant negative relationship between renewable energy consumption in Turkey between 1990-2010. The negative effect of renewable energy consumption is explained by the relatively high cost associated with their adoption and relatively lower role in total energy consumption compared to other energy sources.

Financial Development and Economic Growth

At the same time, research on renewable energy-financial proliferated, providing generally mixed results. De Gregorio & Guidotti (1995) employ the ratio between bank credit to private sector and GDP to measure financial improvements. General sample results demonstrate a positive relationship between financial development and economic growth, yet in country-level analysis, results are different and negative in the case of Latin American countries. Similarly, Demetriades & Hussein (1996) and Ram (1999) observe causal links but state that causality patterns vary widely among the countries. Moreover, the adverse effect of financial development is negative and weak, as confirmed by Ram (1999). Adusei (2013) opposes financial liberalization in Ghana as it may hinder economic growth. An increase in competition will likely result in '…unconventional practices that could have dire consequences for the economy' (p. 70). In Sub-Saharan Africa, financial development also negatively impacts economic growth through large-scale financing of risky and unsustainable investments, increased fuel consumption, and thus accelerating inflation (Ibrahim, M., & Alagidede, 2018).

As opposed to De Gregorio & Guidotti (1995), Adusei (2013) and Ibrahim, M., & Alagidede (2018) researches, a study of Hermes & Lensink (2003) argues that financial development is beneficial for attracting foreign capital inflows and enhancing economic growth using a 67 countries data in 37 of which the positive effect of financial development is especially obvious, including Latin American countries. Calderón & Liu (2003) employ data on 109 developing and industrial countries between 1960-1994 and confirm that in most cases, financial development enhances economic growth, which causes financial development. Moreover, their findings demonstrate that industrial countries benefit more from improvements in their financial systems. Time-series analyses of Liang and Jian-Zhou (2006) confirm a positive relationship between the variables and causality running from economic growth to financial development. They explain that it is critical for China to develop strong financial intermediaries and liberalize interest rates to improve credit allocation. Positive association is also observed in Taiwan (Chang & Caudill, 2005). Hassan et al. (2011) observe a positive link between financial development and economic growth in developing economies between 1980-2007. Financial development, measured by credit to the private sector, liquid liabilities of the banking system, and the ratio of gross domestic savings, facilitate economic development in the middle- and low-income countries. Positive association is also observed in some recent studies (Durusu-Ciftci et al., 2017; Asteriou & Spanos, 2019; Malarvizhi et al., 2019).

Financial Development and Renewable Energy

In light of climate change issues and environmental degradation, research on the financial development-renewables nexus has enlarged recently, yet the evidence is still limited. Kim & Park (2016) reveal that financial development enhances renewable energy consumption using a sample of 30 countries between 2000-2013. Its positive effect is explained by eased access to external funding. Countries with relatively developed financial markets encounter faster renewable energy consumption growth due to renewable technologies mostly dependent on debt and equity financing. Ji & Zhang (2019) explore the relationship in the energy structure of China between 1992-2013. Financial development proxied by the stock market is critical for China to improve the energy structure considering the initial costs and risks associated with adopting renewables. Eren et al. (2019) reveal a statistically significant and positive impact of financial development on economic growth using Indian data for 1971-2015. They also observe unidirectional causality running from financial development to economic growth. Improving the financial system encourages green investments, which leads to significant structural change in some industries, increased public awareness, and higher shares of renewable energy consumption in the longer term. Similary, Pham (2019) confirms the positive effect of financial development on biomass and nonbiomass renewable technologies and explains that its role is more significant in countries with relatively greater carbon intensity and higher growth of innovations. Anton & Afloarei Nucu (2020) investigate the relationship using data on 28 European countries between 1990-2015 using panel data fixed effects estimator. All proxies of financial development (banking sector, bond market, and capital market) are significantly and positively related to renewable energy consumption. The study of Wang et al. (2021) demonstrates that the effect of financial development may vary within the short- and long terms. In the long term, financial development negatively relates to renewable energy consumption, but a positive association arises in the short term. At the same time, some studies demonstrate neither a significant relationship (Assi et al., 2021) nor a causal statistically significant relationship (I. Khan & Hou, 2021).

Data and Model

Our study empirically investigates the link between financial development and renewable energy consumption in Europe and Central Asia. Our sample includes 40[3] Europe and Central Asia between 1995-2015. The reason behind including the abovementioned countries is solely technical. Our methods prefer a strongly balanced dataset, which does not allow us to include countries with data gaps and interpolation may distort the results. Thus, we explore the relationship using 840 observations in total.

Renewable Energy Consumption

The Independent variable of this study is renewable energy consumption, measured as % of total final energy consumption. According to Table 1, it is evident that on average, renewables are not widely consumed by Europe and Central Asia: the average share in total energy consumption is 16%.

Table 1. Summary statistics

Variable	Indicator	Source	Mean	Std. Dev.	Min	Max
RE	Renewable energy consumption (% of total final energy consumption)	WDI	16.22	15.58	0.85	77.34
FD	Financial development index	IMF	0.46	0.25	0.03	1.00
FDI	Foreign direct investment, net inflows (% of GDP)	WDI	6.97	18.95	-15.84	280.13
CO2	CO_2 emissions (metric tons per capita)	WDI	7.18	3.31	0.49	16.42
Y	GDP per capita (constant 2010 US$)	WDI	23788.53	20854.54	534.96	91565.73

---

[3] Albania, Armenia, Austria, Azerbaijan, Belarus, Belgium, Bulgaria, Croatia, Cyprus, Czech Republic, Denmark, Estonia, Finland, France, Germany, Greece, Hungary, Iceland, Ireland, Italy, Kazakhstan, Kyrgyz Republic, Latvia, Lithuania, Moldova, Netherlands, Norway, Poland, Portugal, Romania, Russian Federation, Slovak Republic, Slovenia, Spain, Sweden, Switzerland, Turkey   , Ukraine, United Kingdom, Uzbekistan.

In 2015, major renewable energy consumers were Nordic countries – Iceland (77%), Norway (58%), Sweden (53%), Finland (43%), and Albania (39%). At the bottom of the list are post-Soviet economies, including Ukraine (4%), Russian Federation (3%), Uzbekistan (3%), Azerbaijan (2%), and Kazakhstan (2%). At the same time, between 1995-2015, average renewable energy consumption has been increasing (Figure 1).

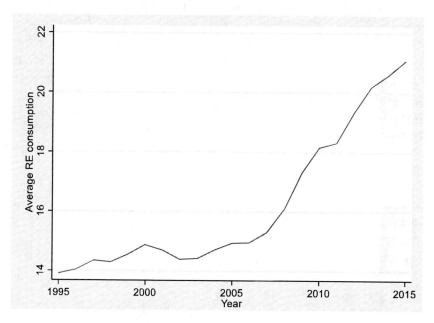

Figure 1. Average renewable energy consumption.

Financial Development Index

Previous empirical studies measure financial development by the share of credit to private sector broad money and stock market capitalization (Hassan et al., 2011; Anton & Afloarei Nucu, 2020; Isaeva et al., 2021), yet such indicators do not reflect the multidimensional nature of financial development. Although the abovementioned proxies are indeed important in the financial development of the economies, some other factors have to be considered as well, such as efficiency and access to financial institutions and markets. Following M. T. I. Khan et al. (2019), we employ a composite index of financial development developed by the International Monetary Fund (IMF)[4] to overcome the shortcoming of employing proxy variables. The index consists of several indices which reflect the development of financial institutions and financial markets in terms of depth, access, and efficiency. Banks, insurance companies, mutual and pension funds are included in financial institutions, and stock and bond markets account for the development of financial markets. Financial development is defined as a combination of depth (size and liquidity of markets), access (the ability of individuals and companies to access financial services), and efficiency (ability of institutions to provide financial services at low cost and with sustainable revenues, and the level of activity of capital markets) (Svirydzenka, 2016). Financial institution and financial markets development indices are then normalized between 0 and 1 and aggregated to higher-level to further make up an overall index. The index covers 183 countries between 1980-2013.

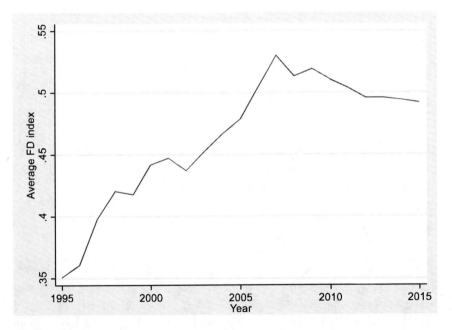

Figure 2. Average financial development.

Our sample's average value of financial development is 0.46 (Table 1), with an increasing trend between 1995-2015 (Figure 2). Between 1995-2008 economies of Europe and Central Asia experienced a rapid increase in the

---

[4] https://data.imf.org/?sk=F8032E80-B36C-43B1-AC26-493C5B1CD33B.

financial development index, yet after the Global Financial Crisis, a downward trend was observed. In 2015, the most financially developed economies were European countries - Switzerland (0.98), Spain (0.89), United Kingdom (0.88), Sweden (0.79), and Italy (0.78), while the most underdeveloped are Albania (0.2), Azerbaijan (0.19), Belarus (0.17), Uzbekistan (0.17) and Kyrgyz Republic (0.12).

Control Variables

Control variables include foreign direct inflows, carbon dioxide emissions in metric tons per capita and per capita economic growth. Average foreign capital inflows in our sample are approximately 7% of GDP. As a result, CO_2 emissions are 7.18 metric tons per person and GDP per capita is 23.8 thousand dollars per capita.

Model

In our study, renewable energy consumption is predicted by the financial development index, foreign capital inflows, carbon dioxide emissions, and per capita economic growth. Therefore, the function can be depicted as follows:

$$RE_{i,t} = f(FD_{i,t}, FDI_{i,t}, CO2_{i,t}, Y_{i,t}) \tag{1}$$

where RE is renewable energy consumption, FD is an index of financial development, FDI is foreign direct inflows, CO2 is carbon dioxide emissions per capita, and Y is the income per capita. i and t represent individual and temporal dimensions. All variables are measured differently and the distribution of several of them requires log transformation. Although logarithmic transformation usually should not be applied to normalized indicators such as the index of financial development, natural log transformation makes all variables follow the same measurement unit (Paramati et al., 2017) and avoid autocorrelation and heteroscedasticity issues (Zafar et al., 2020). Noteworthy, negative values of FDI are eliminated before taking natural logs by shifting the FDI data by the lowest value. After natural log transformation, Eq. 1 is rewritten as follows:

$$\ln RE_{i,t} = \beta_0 + \beta_1 \ln FD_{i,t} + \beta_2 \ln FDI_{i,t} + \beta_3 \ln CO2_{i,t} + \beta_4 Y_{i,t} + \varepsilon_{i,t} \tag{2}$$

Methods

Panel Unit-Root Test

Our analyses start from testing the series for stationarity, which is a common issue in panel data. Moreover, stationarity is crucial when applying the cointegration approach because the cointegrating relationship may exist in a series that is stationary after first-order integration (Pedroni, 1999). We test our variables using three stationarity tests, including the IPS test by (Im et al., 2003) and two Fisher-type tests by (Maddala & Wu, 1999). Under the null hypothesis, the tests assume that panels are stationary.

Pedroni's Panel Cointegration

After checking the integration order, we proceed with the cointegration analysis. For this purpose, we employ a panel cointegration test developed by (Pedroni, 1999). The test checks the hypothesis of non-cointegrating relationship by re-estimating Eq. 2 with seven different test statistics including parametric and non-parametric measures including panel-v, panel-rho, group-rho, panel-t (non-parametric), group-t (non-parametric), panel-ADF (parametric t), and group-ADF (parametric t). Results were derived by aggregating group and panel statistics. Group statistics calculate average results for individual panels, while panel statistics pool the statistic within the dimension (Neal, 2014). The null hypothesis is rejected when most test statistics state a cointegrating relationship. Unlike most cointegration tests, Pedroni's test is one-tailed. We also test for cointegration using the Kao panel cointegration test to measure robustness (Kao, 1999).

Pooled Mean Group Regression

Following Wang et al. (2021), to estimate the short- and long-term coefficients, Pooled Mean Group (PMG) regression introduced by (Pesaran et al., 1999) is employed. PMG estimator transforms the autoregressive distributed lag (ARDL) model parameters to obtain short- and long-term regression coefficients in panel datasets. Regression results allow error correction of cointegrated variables that may deviate from the long-term equilibrium (Blackburne & Frank, 2007). After the transformation regression equation is as follows:

$$\Delta y_{it} = \phi_i\left(y_{i,t-1} - \theta_i' X_{it}\right) + \sum_{j=1}^{p-1} \lambda_{i,j}^* \Delta y_{i,t-1} + \sum_{j=0}^{q-1} \delta_{ij}'^* \Delta X_{i,t-j} + \mu_i + \epsilon_{it}$$

(3)

Applying Eq.3 to our model, y_{it} is RE, x_is are independent variables, $\lambda_{i,j}^*$ and $\delta_{ij}'^*$ are the short-term coefficients, θ_i' is the long-term coefficient, μ_i group-specific effects and ϵ_{it} stochastic error term.

Table 2. Results of unit-root analyses

Form	Variable	Test		
		IPS	ADF Fisher	PP Fisher
Level	ln RE	-5.8773	45.8778	76.5870
		(1.0000)	(0.9992)	(0.5874)
First-difference	Δ ln RE	-13.6550*	340.8946*	785.7304*
		(0.0000)	(0.0000)	(0.0000)
Level	ln FD	-0.1176	27.9596	34.4836
		(0.4532)	(0.8838)	(0.6328)
First-difference	Δ ln FD	-7.9042*	111.2021*	248.9811*
		(0.0000)	(0.0000)	(0.0000)
Level	ln FDI	-6.9548*	155.7378*	228.7883*
		(0.0000)	(0.0000)	(0.0000)
First-difference	Δ ln FDI	-15.8537*	462.9962*	1179.2421*
		(0.0000)	(0.0000)	(0.0000)
Level	ln CO2	4.8799	76.0476	54.8001
		(1.0000)	(0.6044)	(0.9860)
First-difference	Δ ln CO2	-13.8287*	348.5718*	859.2973*
		(0.0000)	(0.0000)	(0.0000)
Level	ln Y	-0.4477	92.6646	109.4198
		(0.3272)	(0.1575)	(0.0161)
First-difference	Δ ln Y	-7.8033*	227.4366*	276.7429*
		(0.0000)	(0.0000)	(0.0000)

* Indicates significance at 1% significance level. Figures in parentheses are p-values.

Results

We first report the results of the panel unit-root test in Table 2. Renewable energy consumption, financial development, carbon emissions, and per capita income are non-stationary under the level form. After first-differencing, however, there is no unit root in the data series at a 1% significance level. The presence of unit root in the majority of the variables and their stationary after the first order differencing satisfies requirements for cointegration analysis.

Table 3 reports the results of Pedroni's panel cointegration. We can see that v-stat, panel PP-stat, panel ADF-stat, group-PP stat, and group-ADF stat reject the null hypothesis of no-cointegration at 1a % significance level, which provides us with enough evidence to state the long-term cointegrating relationship between the variables in our model. Another cointegration test by Kao also confirms cointegration at a 1% significance level.

Table 3. Panel cointegration tests results

Test statistic	Score
V-stat	-2.56***
Panel rho-stat	-0.84
Panel PP-stat	-12.20***
Panel ADF-stat	4.88***
Group rho stat	0.80
Group PP stat	-15.91***
Group ADF stat	7.03***
Kao's ADF	-12.88***

Note: ***, ** and * indicate significance at 1%, 5% and 10% levels, respectively.

Finally, Table 4 reports the results of Pesaran's pooled mean group regression. Again, the effect of the financial development index is intriguing. Financial development is positively related to renewable energy sources' consumption in the long-term at $p < 0.01$. In the short term, however, the effect of financial development turns negative and remains highly significant.

Similar to our long-term results, many studies confirm a positive relationship between renewable energy consumption and financial development (Alsagr & van Hemmen, 2021; Anton & Afloarei Nucu, 2020; Eren et al., 2019; Ji & Zhang, 2019).

Interestingly, Raza et al., (2020) explain that financial development, measured either by financial system deposits, stock market capitalization, or private credit, affects renewable energy consumption differently depending on its initial development. The association is negative in countries with underdeveloped financial systems, while countries with well-developed financial systems enjoy its positive effect on renewable energy consumption.

Table 4. Pesaran's pooled mean group estimator results

Δ ln RE (dependent variable)	Pooled mean group	
Variable	Coefficient	Standard error
Long-term coefficients		
Ln FD	0.1768*** (0.005)	0.06365
ln FDI	0.6845*** (0.000)	0.1314
ln CO2	-1.1157*** (0.000)	0.0838
ln Y	- 0.0842* (0.089)	0.0495
Error correction term	- 0.1689*** (0.001)	0.0518
Δ ln FD	-0.1154*** (0.008)	0.0438
Δ ln FDI	-0.2373 (0.188)	0.1802
Δ ln CO2	-0.5036*** (0.000)	0.1052
Δ ln Y	-0.0867 (0.622)	0.1759
Intercept	0.5990*** (0.000)	0.1499

Note: ***, ** and * indicate significance at 1%, 5% and 10% levels, respectively.

Moreover, such twofold results can remind the logic behind the environmental Kuznets curve and may be explained by the changing priorities of countries within the development course. At the earlier development stages, countries aim to increase welfare, and thus, the developing financial sector may benefit the most income-generating sectors, overlooking the potential of the renewable energy sector. Although financial development plays a significant role in the energy sector (Sadorsky, 2010, 2011), economies may pay more attention to conventional energy sources than renewable energy, especially resource-abundant countries. Some studies demonstrate that financial development increases the traditional demand for energy and promotes industrial development and urbanization, exacerbating environmental pollution (Chang, 2015; Gokmenoglu & Sadeghieh, 2019; Shahbaz & Lean, 2012; Tamazian et al., 2009). Financial development indeed increases the number of activities which increases energy demand (Sadorsky, 2011). Strong financial systems and sustainable financial institutions may attract investment and improve the efficiency of economic activities in the country. Yet, the powers may be directed to fuel-based or so-called "dirty" sectors, which in turn negatively affects the consumption of renewable energy sources.

However, after countries establish their wellbeing, growth orientation replaces with pro-environmental behavior and renewable energy sources become one of the priorities of sustainable development. At the micro-level, private firms are provided with more financial instruments and incentives to invest in clean energy projects and their research and development (Raza et al., 2020). In this sense, mature financial development is essential for improving the environment. It enables attracting green investment, switching to alternative energy sources, and developing instruments for clean energy strategies (e.g., feed-in-tariffs). Moreover, because green energy technologies require significant initial investments, a well-developed financial system expands the access to financial resources to adopt renewable energy sources.

As of control variable, foreign capital investment increases the share of renewables in total energy use in the long-term only. However, a positive association between renewable energy consumption and FDI is also observed in (Amri 2016; Doytch & Narayan, 2016). Being a source of innovation and financing, FDI encourages energy efficiency by discouraging conventional energy sources and promoting renewables.

CO_2 emissions are negatively associated with renewable energy consumption in Europe and Central Asia in both the short- and long terms. Emissions themselves represent a result of industrial and economic activity. Their sign then demonstrates the state's orientation towards environmental quality. In some cases, the growing level of carbon emissions triggers the adoption of clean energy sources because of low environmental quality. However, in our case, increasing CO_2 decreases the shares of renewable energy consumption due to extensive energy generation by burning such exhaustible energy sources as oil, coal, and gas. At this point, it is worth mentioning several major producers from Europe and Central Asia: in 2015, 72% of total energy consumption was formed by fossil fuels. Per capita income is negatively related to renewable energy consumption only in the long-term, although the relationship is relatively weak ($p < 0.1$).

Conclusion

A number of studies attempt to include financial development in the empirical modeling of economic growth, CO2 emissions, deforestation, income inequality, tourism development, and life satisfaction (Calderon & Liu, 2003; Usman & Makhdum, 2021; Law & Tan, 2009). The current study explores the effect of financial development on renewable energy consumption in one sub-region of BRI, namely, Europe and Central Asia, during 1995-2015. Pedroni's cointegration test is employed to reveal the existence of a long-term cointegrating relationship and ARDL-PMG re-estimates the equation to obtain short- and long-term coefficients. Empirical results reveal a negative and significant relationship between financial development and renewable energy consumption in the short term and a positive and significant relationship in the long term. In the short term, countries are growth-oriented and may be focused more on carbon-intensive sectors. In the longer run, however, climate issues and a shortage of natural resources may facilitate the adoption of renewable energy sources.

Our study suggests that policymakers can use a number of tools to promote renewable energy adoption in BRI countries. First, the government can rely on financial incentives to encourage the development green energy sector. For example, tax cuts and other methods may facilitate renewable energy. In addition, low-interest rates, subsidies, and grants are viable solutions to speed up switching to non-fossil fuel use among households and businesses. However, considering significant differences in the levels of renewable energy use in BRI, prospective studies should explore the macroeconomic drivers of green energy use and assess the general population's perceptions of renewable energy adoption.

References

Abokyi, E., Appiah-Konadu, P., Abokyi, F., & Oteng-Abayie, E. F. (2019). Industrial growth and emissions of CO_2 in Ghana: The role of financial development and fossil fuel consumption. *Energy Reports, 5*, 1339–1353. https://doi.org/10.1016/j.egyr.2019.09.002.

Adusei, M. (2013). Financial development and economic growth: Evidence from Ghana. *The International Journal of Business and Finance Research, 7*(5), 61-76.

Alsagr, N., & van Hemmen, S. (2021). The impact of financial development and geopolitical risk on renewable energy consumption: Evidence from emerging markets. *Environmental Science and Pollution Research.* https://doi.org/10.1007/s11356-021-12447-2.

Amri, F. (2016). The relationship amongst energy consumption, foreign direct investment and output in developed and developing Countries. *Renewable and Sustainable Energy Reviews, 64*, 694–702. https://doi.org/10.1016/j.rser.2016.06.065.

Anton, S. G., & Afloarei Nucu, A. E. (2020). The effect of financial development on renewable energy consumption. A panel data approach. *Renewable Energy, 147*, 330–338. https://doi.org/10.1016/j.renene.2019.09.005.

Assi, A. F., Zhakanova Isiksal, A., & Tursoy, T. (2021). Renewable energy consumption, financial development, environmental pollution, and innovations in the ASEAN + 3 group: Evidence from (P-ARDL) model. *Renewable Energy, 165*, 689–700. https://doi.org/10.1016/j.renene.2020.11.052.

Asteriou, D., & Spanos, K. (2019). The relationship between financial development and economic growth during the recent crisis: Evidence from the EU. *Finance Research Letters, 28*, 238-245.

Blackburne, E. F., & Frank, M. W. (2007). Estimation of Nonstationary Heterogeneous Panels. *The Stata Journal, 7*(2), 197–208. https://doi.org/10.1177/1536867X0700700204.

Boutabba, M. A. (2014). The impact of financial development, income, energy and trade on carbon emissions: Evidence from the Indian economy. *Economic Modelling, 40*, 33–41. https://doi.org/10.1016/j.econmod.2014.03.005.

Calderón, C., & Liu, L. (2003). The direction of causality between financial development and economic growth. *Journal of development economics, 72*(1), 321-334.

Chang, S.-C. (2015). Effects of financial developments and income on energy consumption. *International Review of Economics & Finance, 35*, 28–44. https://doi.org/10.1016/j.iref.2014.08.011.

Chang, T., & Caudill*, S. B. (2005). Financial development and economic growth: the case of Taiwan. *Applied economics, 37*(12), 1329-1335.

De Gregorio, J., & Guidotti, P. E. (1995). Financial development and economic growth. *World development, 23*(3), 433-448.

Demetriades, P. O., & Hussein, K. A. (1996). Does financial development cause economic growth? Time-series evidence from 16 countries. *Journal of development Economics, 51*(2), 387-411.

Doytch, N., & Narayan, S. (2016). Does FDI influence renewable energy consumption? An analysis of sectoral FDI impact on renewable and non-renewable industrial energy consumption. *Energy Economics, 54*, 291–301. https://doi.org/10.1016/j.eneco.2015.12.010.

Durusu-Ciftci, D., Ispir, M. S., & Yetkiner, H. (2017). Financial development and economic growth: Some theory and more evidence. *Journal of policy modeling, 39*(2), 290-306.

Eren, B. M., Taspinar, N., & Gokmenoglu, K. K. (2019). The impact of financial development and economic growth on renewable energy consumption: Empirical analysis of India. *Science of The Total Environment, 663*, 189–197. https://doi.org/10.1016/j.scitotenv.2019.01.323.

Gokmenoglu, K. K., & Sadeghieh, M. (2019). Financial Development, CO2 Emissions, Fossil Fuel Consumption and Economic Growth: The Case of Turkey. *Strategic Planning for Energy and the Environment, 38*(4), 7–28. https://doi.org/10.1080/10485236.2019.12054409.

Haseeb, M., Abidin, I. S. Z., Hye, Q. M. A., & Hartani, N. H. (2018). The Impact of Renewable Energy on Economic Well-Being of Malaysia: Fresh Evidence from Auto

Regressive Distributed Lag Bound Testing Approach. *International Journal of Energy Economics and Policy, 9*(1), 269–275.

Hassan, M. K., Sanchez, B., & Yu, J.-S. (2011). Financial development and economic growth: New evidence from panel data. *The Quarterly Review of Economics and Finance, 51*(1), 88–104. https://doi.org/10.1016/j.qref.2010.09.001.

Hermes, N., & Lensink, R. (2003). Foreign direct investment, financial development and economic growth. *The journal of development studies, 40*(1), 142-163.

Ibrahim, M., & Alagidede, P. (2018). Effect of financial development on economic growth in sub-Saharan Africa. *Journal of Policy Modeling, 40*(6), 1104-1125.

Im, K. S., Pesaran, M. H., & Shin, Y. (2003). Testing for unit roots in heterogeneous panels. *Journal of Econometrics, 115*(1), 53–74. https://doi.org/10.1016/S0304-4076(03)00092-7.

Isaeva, A., Salahodjaev, R., Khachaturov, A., & Tosheva, S. (2021). The Impact of Tourism and Financial Development on Energy Consumption and Carbon Dioxide Emission: Evidence from Post-communist Countries. *Journal of the Knowledge Economy.* https://doi.org/10.1007/s13132-021-00732-x.

Islam, F., Shahbaz, M., Ahmed, A. U., & Alam, Md. M. (2013). Financial development and energy consumption nexus in Malaysia: A multivariate time series analysis. *Economic Modelling, 30*, 435–441. https://doi.org/10.1016/j.econmod.2012.09.033.

Janpolat, K., Odilova, S., Nodira, A., Salahodjaev, R., & Khachaturov, A. (2021). Financial Development and Energy Consumption Nexus In 32 Belt and Road Economies. *International Journal of Energy Economics and Policy, 11*(2), 368–373. https://doi.org/10.32479/ijeep.10862.

Ji, Q., & Zhang, D. (2019). How much does financial development contribute to renewable energy growth and upgrading of energy structure in China? *Energy Policy, 128*, 114–124. https://doi.org/10.1016/j.enpol.2018.12.047

Kahia, M., Aïssa, M. S. B., & Lanouar, C. (2017). Renewable and non-renewable energy use - economic growth nexus: The case of MENA Net Oil Importing Countries. *Renewable and Sustainable Energy Reviews, 71*, 127–140. https://doi.org/10.1016/j.rser.2017.01.010

Kao, C. (1999). Spurious regression and residual-based tests for cointegration in panel data. *Journal of Econometrics, 90*(1), 1–44. https://doi.org/10.1016/S0304-4076(98)00023-2.

Khan, I., & Hou, F. (2021). The Impact of Socio-economic and Environmental Sustainability on CO_2 Emissions: A Novel Framework for Thirty IEA Countries. *Social Indicators Research*, 1–32. https://doi.org/10.1007/s11205-021-02629-3.

Khan, M. T. I., Yaseen, M. R., & Ali, Q. (2019). Nexus between financial development, tourism, renewable energy, and greenhouse gas emission in high-income countries: A continent-wise analysis. *Energy Economics, 83*, 293–310. https://doi.org/10.1016/j.eneco.2019.07.018.

Kim, J., & Park, K. (2016). Financial development and deployment of renewable energy technologies. *Energy Economics, 59*, 238–250. https://doi.org/10.1016/j.eneco.2016.08.012.

Law, S. H., & Tan, H. B. (2009). The role of financial development on income inequality in Malaysia. *Journal of Economic Development, 34*(2), 153.

Liang, Q., & Jian-Zhou, T. (2006). Financial development and economic growth: Evidence from China. *China economic review*, *17*(4), 395-411.

Lin, B., & Moubarak, M. (2014). Renewable energy consumption – Economic growth nexus for China. *Renewable and Sustainable Energy Reviews, 40*, 111–117. https://doi.org/10.1016/j.rser.2014.07.128.

Maddala, G. S., & Wu, S. (1999). A Comparative Study of Unit Root Tests with Panel Data and a New Simple Test. *Oxford Bulletin of Economics and Statistics, 61*(S1), 631–652. https://doi.org/10.1111/1468-0084.0610s1631.

Malarvizhi, C. A. N., Zeynali, Y., Mamun, A. A., & Ahmad, G. B. (2019). Financial development and economic growth in ASEAN-5 countries. *Global Business Review, 20*(1), 57-71.

Neal, T. (2014). Panel Cointegration Analysis with Xtpedroni. *The Stata Journal, 14*(3), 684–692. https://doi.org/10.1177/1536867X1401400312.

Ntanos, S., Skordoulis, M., Kyriakopoulos, G., Arabatzis, G., Chalikias, M., Galatsidas, S., Batzios, A., & Katsarou, A. (2018). Renewable Energy and Economic Growth: Evidence from European Countries. *Sustainability, 10*(8), 2626. https://doi.org/10.3390/su10082626.

Ocal, O., & Aslan, A. (2013). Renewable energy consumption–economic growth nexus in Turkey. *Renewable and Sustainable Energy Reviews, 28*, 494–499. https://doi.org/10.1016/j.rser.2013.08.036.

Omri, A., Ben Mabrouk, N., & Sassi-Tmar, A. (2015). Modeling the causal linkages between nuclear energy, renewable energy and economic growth in developed and developing countries. *Renewable and Sustainable Energy Reviews, 42*, 1012–1022. https://doi.org/10.1016/j.rser.2014.10.046.

Ozcan, B., & Ozturk, I. (2019). Renewable energy consumption-economic growth nexus in emerging countries: A bootstrap panel causality test. *Renewable and Sustainable Energy Reviews, 104*, 30–37. https://doi.org/10.1016/j.rser.2019.01.020.

Pao, H.-T., & Fu, H.-C. (2013). Renewable energy, non-renewable energy and economic growth in Brazil. *Renewable and Sustainable Energy Reviews, 25*, 381–392. https://doi.org/10.1016/j.rser.2013.05.004.

Paramati, S. R., Shahbaz, M., & Alam, Md. S. (2017). Does tourism degrade environmental quality? A comparative study of Eastern and Western European Union. Transportation Research Part D: *Transport and Environment, 50*, 1–13. https://doi.org/10.1016/j.trd.2016.10.034.

Pedroni, P. (1999). Critical Values for Cointegration Tests in Heterogeneous Panels with Multiple Regressors. *Oxford Bulletin of Economics and Statistics, 61*(S1), 653–670. https://doi.org/10.1111/1468-0084.0610s1653.

Pesaran, M. H., Shin, Y., & Smith, R. P. (1999). Pooled Mean Group Estimation of Dynamic Heterogeneous Panels. *Journal of the American Statistical Association, 94*(446), 621–634. https://doi.org/10.1080/01621459.1999.10474156.

Pham, L. (2019). Does financial development matter for innovation in renewable energy? Applied *Economics Letters, 26*(21), 1756–1761. https://doi.org/10.1080/13504851.2019.1593934.

Rahman, M. M., & Velayutham, E. (2020). Renewable and non-renewable energy consumption-economic growth nexus: New evidence from South Asia. *Renewable Energy, 147*, 399–408. https://doi.org/10.1016/j.renene.2019.09.007.

Ram, R. (1999). Financial development and economic growth: Additional evidence. *The Journal of Development Studies, 35* (4), 164-174.

Raza, S. A., Shah, N., Qureshi, M. A., Qaiser, S., Ali, R., & Ahmed, F. (2020). Non-linear threshold effect of financial development on renewable energy consumption: Evidence from panel smooth transition regression approach. *Environmental Science and Pollution Research, 27*(25), 32034–32047. https://doi.org/10.1007/s11356-020-09520-7.

Sadorsky, P. (2010). The impact of financial development on energy consumption in emerging economies. *Energy Policy, 38*(5), 2528–2535. https://doi.org/10.1016/j.enpol.2009.12.048.

Sadorsky, P. (2011). Financial development and energy consumption in Central and Eastern European frontier economies. *Energy Policy, 39*(2), 999–1006. https://doi.org/10.1016/j.enpol.2010.11.034.

Salman, D. M., & Atya, E. (2014). What is the role of Financial Development and Energy Consumption on Economic Growth? *International Journal of Finance & Banking Studies* (2147-4486), 3(1), 137–149. https://doi.org/10.20525/ijfbs.v3i1.175.

Shahbaz, M., & Lean, H. H. (2012). Does financial development increase energy consumption? The role of industrialization and urbanization in Tunisia. *Energy Policy, 40*, 473–479. https://doi.org/10.1016/j.enpol.2011.10.050.

Shahbaz, M., Raghutla, C., Chittedi, K. R., Jiao, Z., & Vo, X. V. (2020). The effect of renewable energy consumption on economic growth: Evidence from the renewable energy country attractive index. *Energy, 207*, 118162. https://doi.org/10.1016/j.energy.2020.118162.

Svirydzenka, K. (2016). Introducing a New Broad-Based Index of Financial Development (SSRN Scholarly Paper ID 2754950). *Social Science Research Network.* https://papers.ssrn.com/abstract=2754950.

Tamazian, A., Chousa, J. P., & Vadlamannati, K. C. (2009). Does higher economic and financial development lead to environmental degradation: Evidence from BRIC countries. *Energy Policy, 37*(1), 246–253. https://doi.org/10.1016/j.enpol.2008.08.025.

Usman, M., & Makhdum, M. S. A. (2021). What abates ecological footprint in BRICS-T region? Exploring the influence of renewable energy, non-renewable energy, agriculture, forest area and financial development. *Renewable Energy, 179*, 12-28.

Wang, J., Zhang, S., & Zhang, Q. (2021). The relationship of renewable energy consumption to financial development and economic growth in China. *Renewable Energy, 170*, 897–904. https://doi.org/10.1016/j.renene.2021.02.038.

Zafar, M. W., Shahbaz, M., Sinha, A., Sengupta, T., & Qin, Q. (2020). How renewable energy consumption contribute to environmental quality? The role of education in OECD countries. *Journal of Cleaner Production, 268*, 122149. https://doi.org/10.1016/j.jclepro.2020.122149.

Chapter 4

Institutions and Quality of Life

Raufhon Salahodjaev[*]

Tashkent State University of Economics, Tashkent, Uzbekistan

Abstract

The aim of this study is to explore the relationship between institutions and quality of life over the period 1990-2019. Our empirical results suggest that there is significant positive link between governance and wellbeing of society. For example, 1 standard deviation increase in quality of governance is associated with slightly less than half-standard deviation increases in SWB. We also find that life satisfaction decreases with a reduction in employment rates. For example, 10 percentage points increase in unemployment rates is associated with 0.6 points increase in LS.

Keywords: governance, life satisfaction, longevity

Introduction and Review of Related Literature

The goals of policymakers in Belt Road Initiative (BRI) countries strive to not only increase economic progress but also to improve quality of life. Ample evidence indicates that income, demographic transitions, and human capital play a significant role in achieving that objective (Boyce et al., 2010; Nikolaev

---

[*] Corresponding Author's Email: Salahodjaev@gmail.com.

In: Economic Growth and Wellbeing
Editor: Raufhon Salahodjaev
ISBN: 978-1-68507-990-1

and Salahodjaev, 2016). At the same time, growing research evidence suggests that governance is one of the variables related to various quality of life indicators (Nikolova, 2016). This study aims to contribute to this strand of research by exploring the relationship between governance and quality of life. First, we focus on a group of countries engaged in the BRI over the period between 1990-2019. Second, we use a wide range of governance indicators compiled by the World Bank to capture complex interrelations in the institutions and quality of life nexus. Third, we use two proxies for quality of life: life satisfaction index and life expectancy at birth. The life satisfaction index is one of the most widely used proxies for well-being in extant research (McCulloch, 1992). Life expectancy at birth indicates the number of years a newborn would live if prevailing patterns of mortality at the time of their birth were to stay the same throughout their life[1]. Therefore, these two variables can capture our sample's overall level of quality of life.

Institutions[2] and Life Satisfaction

The research on the relationship between institutions and life satisfaction can be divided into several strands. First group of studies explores the relationship between worldwide governance indicators and life satisfaction. Helliwell and Huang (2008) use six governance indicators from the World Bank dataset and life satisfaction scores from World Values Survey on 75 nations for the years 1981-2000 to explore the relationship between good governance and SWB. The results suggest that the overall governance index is positively linked to SWB even when the authors split data into sub-samples. Moreover, governance reduces suicide rates and improves SWB even after accounting for quality of health, social trust, and religiosity. In addition, economic freedom is one of the facets of governance quality that has been explored in happiness research. Economic freedom encompasses ease of entrepreneurship, elimination of trade restrictions, capital movements and labor freedom, promotion of competition, and efficiency of the legal system. All these aspects should be linked to higher life satisfaction. For instance, Graafland and Compen (2015), using data for 120 countries over the years 2007-2009, found that various dimensions of economic freedom are significantly related to life satisfaction. Moreover, GDP per capita and trust mediate the relationship

---

[1] https://data.worldbank.org/indicator/SP.DYN.LE00.IN.
[2] We use institutions and governance interchangeably in this study.

between the quality of the legal system and SWB. Graafland and Lous (2018) explore the relationship between income inequality, economic freedom, and life satisfaction in a sample of 21 OECD nations. The empirical findings suggest that income inequality moderates the relationship between economic freedom and SWB. Furthermore, Spruk and Kešeljević (2016) rely on World Database on Happiness to explore the relationship between economic freedom and life satisfaction in a sample of 139 countries for the years 1996-2010. Using a wide range of estimation methods such as OLS and EBA, the study confirms that people living in countries with higher economic freedom scores are more likely to report higher levels of life satisfaction. Moreover, this effect is independent of social capital and economic development.

Liu et al., (2020) explore the relationship between quality of government and life satisfaction using sub-national data from China. The data obtained by phone interviews on a sample of 5015 respondents shows that delivering public services efficiently, timely and with high quality has a significant positive influence on residential life satisfaction. Therefore, trust in the government is an essential tool to promote quality of life along the path of economic development. In a similar study, based on data from China, Yu et al., (2011) explore the relationship between satisfaction with local government and life satisfaction across 21 cities between 2004-2010. The regression modeling results suggest that life satisfaction is positively correlated with income and satisfaction with the government. More precisely, satisfaction with the government increases with the rise in income. Corruption is one of the dimensions of institutional quality that has been linked to life satisfaction. Ciziceno and Travaglino (2019) stress that a lack of efficient corruption policies can increase income inequality and reduce economic growth. Using different data from the USA and the MENA regions, the study conjectures that institutional trust is an important variable mediating the link between governance and life satisfaction. The empirical results suggest that corruption has both direct and indirect effects (via trust) on SWB.

Another study focuses on institutional reforms in Latin America and their effects on life satisfaction (Machia & Plagnol, 2019). The authors use Gallup World data for the years 2009-2016 to explore the relationship between confidence in various national institutions and life satisfaction. The study shows that confidence in institutions positively correlates with life satisfaction. Therefore, the study highlights the importance of institutional reforms to improve the quality of life in Latin America. In a different study, Rodrigues-Pose and Maslauskaite (2012) estimate the life satisfaction model is conditional on personal, socio-economic, and institutional factors using data for Central and Eastern European countries.

Another aspect of research explores the effect of various economic institutions on SWB. For example, Ochsen and Welsch (2012), using data for more than 350,000 respondents across 10 countries in the EU for the years 1975-2002, explore the relationship between employment protection legislature and SWB. This study finds that labor market protection dimensions have benefits that exceed beyond social welfare. In particular, higher levels of employment protection have positive effects on life satisfaction. Moreover, unemployment insurance is also found to be positively linked to SWB. Jakubow (2014) introduces the role of governance in the ongoing debate on the effects of state intervention on life satisfaction, using data for 15 developed countries between 2005-2008. The results suggest that a rise in government support relative to GDP positively correlates with SWB. Moreover, the quality of institutions further increases this positive association. Thus, the institutional environment moderates the relationship between public resources allocation and life satisfaction. In a more recent study, Salahodjaev (2015) argues that quality of governance is important in the tolerance-SWB nexus. Using data for 81 countries, the author finds that once the quality of governance index is considered, tolerance is insignificantly related to happiness inequality. The author argues that tolerant societies are more likely to build more efficient and accountable institutions, which in turn affects SWB.

Institutions and Life Expectancy

The research on the life expectancy drivers has grown considerably over the past two decades (Shaw, 2005; Sede and Ohemeng, 2015; Lin et al., 2012). These studies have also considered the role of institutional indicators. For example, Stroup (2007) contributes to the debate on the relationship between economic freedom and life expectancy by arguing that democratization is a variable that has been overlooked by extant research. Using data for up to 105 nations, the study interacts economic freedom index and political rights index. The results from empirical modeling suggest that economic liberties enhance health in countries with higher levels of democratization. Gropper et al., (2011) explore the relationship between GDP per capita, economic freedom, happy life years, and life satisfaction across more than 100 nations.

The empirical analysis suggests that economic freedom and GDP per capita have a significant and positive relationship with well-being. In addition, a simultaneous increase in GDP and economic freedom in low-income countries make a considerable boost in well-being.

Hauck et al., (2016) investigated the socio-economic determinants of longevity across 54 less developed countries from 1990 through 2012. Using Extreme Bound Analysis, the study finds that life expectancy is predicted by HIV rates, gender equality, agriculture, human capital, and political stability. In addition, the results suggest that quality of governance is among the robust determinants of life expectancy. In a more recent study, Islam et al., (2018) explore the drivers of longevity in low and lower-middle-income countries. The authors find that economic and press freedoms are positively correlated with healthy life expectancy along with other socio-economic variables. In addition, the study highlights the importance of investment in human capital and urbanization to increase longevity.

Makuta and O'Hare (2015) explore the relationship between quality of governance and life expectancy accounting for the public spending on health, using data from 43 Sub-Saharan Africa countries between 1996 and 2011. The two-stage least squares regression results suggest that public spending on health increases life expectancy and reduces mortality. Moreover, this effect is stronger in countries with a higher quality of institutions. Ibrahim and Ajide (2021) examined the relationship between energy use, income, and life expectancy in four African countries (Algeria, Egypt, Libya, and Nigeria) between 1990-2017. The study uses cointegration, unit root, and other methods to model the relationship. The results suggest that the quality of institutions moderate the relationship between income and life expectancy.

In contrast, Kireenko and Nevzorova (2015) test the hypothesis that market failures may influence the quality of life. Data of 150 nations collected between 1999-2007 explores the relationship between shadow economy and longevity. The cluster analysis and regression modeling show that life expectancy is inversely related to the size of the shadow economy. Feyzabadi et al., (2015), using data for 158 nations from 2007 to 2012, explore the relationship between peace and life expectancy. The authors rely on Global Peace Index in the linear regression modeling controlling for the economic development and human development index. The findings suggest that peace, a proxy for the stability of national institutions, is positively related to life expectancy. Young (2001) looks from a different aspect on the institutions-longevity nexus. In particular, the author considers the impact of gendered institutions on life expectancy across less developed economies. The results suggest that pluralism and gendered institutions positively influence average national life expectancy levels.

Data and Methodology

We use two proxies for quality of life. Our first proxy is the life satisfaction index that has been widely used in extant research to understand the individual and cross-country differences in subjective well-being. Our life satisfaction (LS) index comes from World Happiness Report. The data spans from 2005 to 2019. Our second proxy is life expectancy (LE) from the World Bank. We use the data for longevity as an alternative to LS as they are positively correlated ($r = .55$; $p = 0.00$), and the data for longevity is available from 1990 to 2019.

Our main independent variable is Governance Index (GI), estimated from 6 Worldwide Governance Indicators available in the World Bank Data portal. These 6 dimensions are Rule of Law (ROL), Control of Corruption (COR), Regulatory Quality (RQ), Government Effectiveness (GE), Political Stability (PS), and Voice and Accountability (VA) indicators. The GI is predicted from the principal component analysis in Stata 16. This index ranges from -6 to +6, where higher values reflect more efficient governance.

We estimate the following equations to assess the relationship between governance and quality of life:

$$LS = a_0 + a_1 GDP + a_2 GI + a_3 UNEMPL + a_4 WP + a_5 SOCIAL + a_6 AGE + \varepsilon \quad (1)$$

$$LE = a_0 + a_1 GDP + a_2 GI + a_3 HIV + a_4 WP + a_5 AGE + \varepsilon \quad (2)$$

where LS is life satisfaction index, LE is life expectancy, GI is governance index, UNEMPL is the unemployment rate, WP is the share of women in parliament, SOCIAL is social support index, AGE is age dependency ration, and ε is an error term. We estimate Eq. (1) and Eq. (2) using a fixed-effects regression estimator. We include the abovementioned control factors to reduce the omitted variable bias. The descriptive statistics are reported in Table 1.

Table 1. Descriptive statistics

Variable	Description	Mean	Std. Dev.	Min	Max
LS	Life Satisfaction Index	5.34	0.81	2.38	7.60
LE	Life expectancy at birth, total (years)	70.86	5.58	50.33	83.15
Governance	Quality of Governance Index	0.00	2.20	-5.25	5.72
GDP	GDP per capita, PPP (constant 2017 international $)	17.71	18.20	0.61	111.45
Unemployment	Unemployment, total (% of total labor force) (modeled ILO estimate)	7.84	6.49	0.39	37.25
Parliament	Proportion of seats held by women in national parliaments (%)	13.99	9.40	0.00	50.00
Social	Social Support Index	0.82	0.10	0.37	0.99
Age	Age dependency ratio (% of working-age population)	56.38	16.68	16.07	117.88
HIV	Prevalence of HIV, total (% of population ages 15-49)	0.24	0.31	0.10	2.20

Empirical Results

We start from a visual representation of the relationship between GDP per capita (income) and life satisfaction for BRI countries for 2019 (Figure 1). The results confirm that there is a positive relationship between economic development and subjective wellbeing (SWB). Therefore, it is important to start the empirical modeling by including the GDP per capita. The results are reported in Table 2. Column 1 offers bivariate regression between LS and GDP per capita. As expected, the coefficient is positive and significant, suggesting that economic progress improves SWB. In column 2, we introduce the governance index to test whether there is a direct relationship between governance in LS. Again, we find that both governance and GDP per capita are positive and significant. For example, 1 standard deviation increase in quality of governance is associated with slightly less than half-standard deviation increases in SWB.

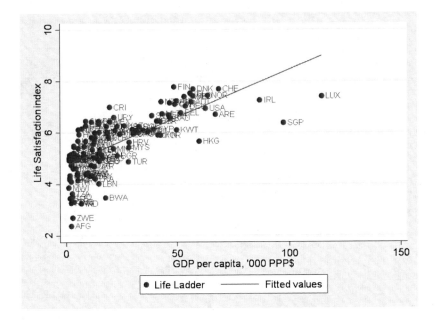

Figure 1. Scatterplot between life satisfaction and GDP per capita, 2019.

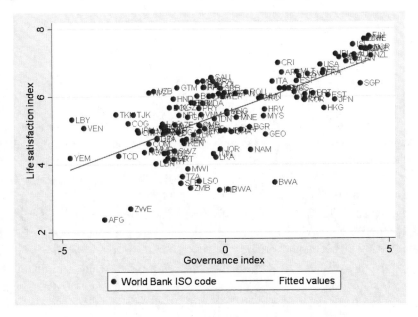

Figure 2. Scatterplot between Governance index and Life satisfaction.

In order to reduce the omitted variable bias, we introduce a set of control variables in columns 3-6. We include the unemployment rate to assess the relationship between labor market conditions and well-being. Life satisfaction decreases with a reduction in employment rates. For example, 10 percentage points increase in unemployment rates is associated with 0.6 points increase in LS. We additionally add a share of women in parliament (column 4), as research suggests that female political empowerment is linked to life satisfaction (Salahodjaev et al., 2020). While the representation of women in parliament is insignificant in our regression, the estimate for governance is unaffected. We include social support (column 5) and age dependency ratio (column 6). These two variables are positively related to SWB. Therefore, we further confirm that social capital is an important antecedent of life satisfaction. Turning to our main variable of interest, governance overall positively affects life satisfaction after controlling for other socio-economic outcomes.

We then test separate effects of governance sub-indexes on life satisfaction (Table 3). In particular, we include ROL, COR, RQ, GE, PS, and VA indicators. Of these indicators, ROL, GE, and PS are positively and significantly related to SWB. For example, if ROL increases from the level of Mongolia to Estonia for the year 2019, life satisfaction will increase by 0.237 points. At the same time, regulatory quality, voice and accountability, and control of corruption are not significantly linked to SWB in BRI countries.

Table 4 further explores the relationship between overall governance and life expectancy. The results in column 5 are similar to the findings in Table 3. We find that a one-point increase in the GI is associated with 0.23 years increase in overall life expectancy. Our estimated results also suggest that economic progress and representation of women in parliament are positively linked to longevity in Belt Road Initiative countries. The importance of female political empowerment is also confirmed by Mirziyoyeva and Salahodjaev (2021) in the context of the overall SDG agenda. Additionally, we test separate effects of GI on LE as performed in Table 3. Overall, we also find mixed results in Table 5. ROL, RQ, and GE are positively related to LE. For example, a 1-point increase in ROL is associated with 0.6 years increase in longevity. In contrast, VA is negatively correlated to LE, while PS and COR are insignificant in our empirical analysis. Therefore, the results in Table 5 suggest a complex relationship between governance and LE in BRI.

Table 2. Baseline results: life satisfaction

	I	II	III	IV	V	VI
GDP	0.039	0.034	0.019	0.018	0.016	0.014
	$(8.31)^{***}$	$(6.83)^{***}$	$(3.88)^{***}$	$(3.62)^{***}$	$(3.36)^{***}$	$(2.80)^{***}$
Governance		0.162	0.140	0.131	0.126	0.142
		$(3.54)^{***}$	$(3.24)^{***}$	$(2.97)^{***}$	$(2.97)^{***}$	$(3.37)^{***}$
Unemployment			-0.056	-0.055	-0.045	-0.042
			$(8.59)^{***}$	$(8.52)^{***}$	$(7.18)^{***}$	$(6.69)^{***}$
Parliament				0.004	0.004	0.005
				(1.19)	(1.14)	(1.37)
Support					2.296	2.149
					$(7.76)^{***}$	$(7.26)^{***}$
Age						0.015
						$(3.51)^{***}$
Constant	4.553	4.654	5.397	5.339	3.430	2.819
	$(46.21)^{***}$	$(45.78)^{***}$	$(41.73)^{***}$	$(38.61)^{***}$	$(12.26)^{***}$	$(8.61)^{***}$
R^2	0.10	0.12	0.21	0.22	0.29	0.30
N	671	671	671	671	666	666

$^*p < 0.1$; $^{**}p < 0.05$; $^{***}p < 0.01$.

Table 3. Subdimensions of governance and life satisfaction

	I	II	III	IV	V	VI
GDP	0.014	0.017	0.018	0.016	0.015	0.018
	(2.93)***	(3.56)***	(3.67)***	(3.30)***	(3.20)***	(3.73)***
Unemployment	-0.043	-0.044	-0.044	-0.044	-0.037	-0.043
	(6.84)***	(6.85)***	(6.83)***	(6.90)***	(5.98)***	(6.82)***
Parliament	0.005	0.006	0.007	0.004	0.008	0.007
	(1.63)	(1.78)*	(1.99)**	(1.17)	(2.35)**	(1.97)**
Support	2.107	2.187	2.193	2.162	2.218	2.193
	(7.04)***	(7.33)***	(7.35)***	(7.27)***	(7.66)***	(7.34)***
Age	0.014	0.014	0.013	0.013	0.018	0.013
	(3.32)***	(3.11)***	(3.08)***	(3.07)***	(4.28)***	(3.07)***
ROL	0.237					
	(2.36)**					
COR		0.072				
		(0.79)				
RQ			-0.026			
			(0.29)			
GE				0.218		
				(2.53)**		
PS					0.280	
					(6.18)***	
VA						-0.011
						(0.12)
Constant	2.902	2.810	2.765	2.877	2.559	2.766
	(8.70)***	(8.40)***	(8.37)***	(8.68)***	(7.95)***	(8.38)***
R^2	0.29	0.29	0.29	0.30	0.33	0.29
N	666	666	666	666	666	666

* $p < 0.1$; ** $p < 0.05$; *** $p < 0.01$.

Table 4. Baseline results: life expectancy

	I	II	III	IV	V
HIV	6.517	4.006	2.595	0.703	0.869
	(11.12)***	(5.64)***	(4.00)***	(1.29)	(1.93)*
Governance		0.487	0.319	0.233	0.230
		(3.40)***	(2.32)**	(1.90)*	(2.26)**
GDP			0.175	0.132	0.123
			(11.98)***	(11.07)***	(12.42)***
Parliament				0.203	0.126
				(20.63)***	(13.77)***
Age					-0.154
					(18.39)***
Constant	68.504	70.009	67.721	66.065	75.542
	(434.23)***	(316.65)***	(230.80)***	(245.08)***	(134.46)***
R^2	0.10	0.06	0.21	0.49	0.65
N	1,123	884	854	783	783

* $p < 0.1$; ** $p < 0.05$; *** $p < 0.01$.

Table 5. Subdimensions of governance and life expectancy

	I	II	III	IV	V	VI
HIV	0.831 (1.84)*	0.962 (2.15)**	0.878 (1.98)**	0.915 (2.11)**	1.105 (2.50)**	1.646 (3.52)***
GDP	0.119 (11.73)***	0.127 (13.00)***	0.118 (11.83)***	0.119 (12.29)***	0.126 (12.89)***	0.126 (12.99)***
Parliament	0.127 (13.88)***	0.125 (13.53)***	0.127 (13.94)***	0.120 (13.12)***	0.128 (13.91)***	0.127 (14.00)***
Age	-0.155 (18.54)***	-0.155 (18.43)***	-0.151 (18.04)***	-0.150 (18.04)***	-0.154 (18.26)***	-0.148 (17.27)***
ROL	0.622 (2.54)**					
COR		0.366 (1.64)				
RQ			0.700 (3.10)***			
GE				1.251 (5.32)***		
PS					-0.021 (0.17)	
VA						-0.824 (3.32)***
Constant	75.773 (130.52)***	75.568 (131.63)***	75.446 (136.37)***	75.503 (138.26)***	75.323 (135.62)***	74.538 (124.24)***
R^2	0.65	0.65	0.65	0.66	0.65	0.65
N	783	783	783	783	783	783

* $p < 0.1$; ** $p < 0.05$; *** $p < 0.01$.

Conclusion and Policy Implications

This study explored the relationship between governance indicators and quality of life in Belt and Road Initiative countries over the years 1990-2019. We have constructed an overall GI using principal component analysis from six governance dimensions. In addition, we used the fixed effects regression estimator to model the relationship between governance and quality of life.

Our empirical results suggest that GI is positively related to LS and LE. For example, a one-point increase in the GI is associated with 0.23 years increase in overall life expectancy. However, the analysis for sub-dimensions of governance has produced mixed results. While ROL, GE, and PS are positively and significantly related to LS, ROL, RQ, GE are positively associated with LE. Moreover, the impact changes across various dimensions of governance. We also find that economic progress has a positive influence on longevity and life satisfaction.

Our study offers several policy implications. First, BRI countries should reform and increase the quality of institutions to improve their quality of life. For example, the rule of law and government efficiency are among two important variables that are positively linked to both LE and LS. The existing evidence suggests that promoting e-governance and improving the delivery of public services in remote areas can increase both qualities of governance and raise overall life satisfaction. In addition, government effectiveness can be improved by increasing the process of automated public services, reducing the reporting layers, and outsourcing some of the services to the private sector. Overall, BRI should establish solid legal and effective institutions where citizens and economic agents can operate and benefit from economic progress.

References

Boyce, C. J., Brown, G. D., & Moore, S. C. (2010). Money and happiness: Rank of income, not income, affects life satisfaction. *Psychological science*, 21(4), 471-475.

Ciziceno, M., & Travaglino, G. A. (2019). Perceived corruption and individuals' life satisfaction: The mediating role of institutional trust. *Social Indicators Research*, 141(2), 685-701.

Feyzabadi, V. Y., Haghdoost, A., Mehrolhassani, M. H., & Aminian, Z. (2015). The association between peace and life expectancy: An empirical study of the world countries. *Iranian journal of public health*, 44(3), 341.

Graafland, J., & Compen, B. (2015). Economic freedom and life satisfaction: Mediation by income per capita and generalized trust. *Journal of Happiness Studies*, 16(3), 789-810.

Graafland, J., & Lous, B. (2018). Economic freedom, income inequality and life satisfaction in OECD countries. *Journal of Happiness Studies*, 19(7), 2071-2093.

Gropper, D. M., Lawson, R. A., & Thorne Jr, J. T. (2011). Economic freedom and happiness. *Cato J.*, 31, 237.

Hauck, K., Martin, S., & Smith, P. C. (2016). Priorities for action on the social determinants of health: Empirical evidence on the strongest associations with life expectancy in 54 low-income countries, 1990–2012. *Social Science & Medicine*, 167, 88-98.

Helliwell, J. F., & Huang, H. (2008). How's your government? International evidence linking good government and well-being. *British journal of political science*, 38(4), 595-619.

Ibrahim, R. L., & Ajide, K. B. (2021). The role of income level and institutional quality in the non-renewable energy consumption and life expectancy nexus: evidence from selected oil-producing economies in Africa. *OPEC Energy Review*, 45(3), 341-364.

Islam, M. S., Mondal, M. N. I., Tareque, M. I., Rahman, M. A., Hoque, M. N., Ahmed, M. M., & Khan, H. T. (2018). Correlates of healthy life expectancy in low-and lower-middle-income countries. *BMC public health*, 18(1), 1-11.

Jakubow, A. (2014). State intervention and life satisfaction reconsidered: The role of governance quality and resource misallocation. *Politics & Policy*, 42(1), 3-36.

Kireenko, A., & Nevzorova, E. (2015). Impact of shadow economy on quality of life: Indicators and model selection. *Procedia Economics and Finance*, 25, 559-568.

Lin, R. T., Chen, Y. M., Chien, L. C., & Chan, C. C. (2012). Political and social determinants of life expectancy in less developed countries: a longitudinal study. *BMC Public Health*, 12(1), 1-8.

Liu, H., Gao, H., & Huang, Q. (2020). Better government, happier residents? Quality of government and life satisfaction in China. *Social Indicators Research*, 147(3), 971-990.

Macchia, L., & Plagnol, A. C. (2019). Life satisfaction and confidence in national institutions: evidence from South America. *Applied Research in Quality of Life*, 14(3), 721-736.

Makuta, I., & O'Hare, B. (2015). Quality of governance, public spending on health and health status in Sub Saharan Africa: a panel data regression analysis. *BMC public health*, 15(1), 1-11.

McCulloch, B. J. (1992). Gender and race: An interaction affecting the replicability of well-being across groups. *Women & Health*, 19, 65-89.

Mirziyoyeva, Z., & Salahodjaev, R. (2021). Women's Parliamentary Representation and Sustainable Development Goals: a Cross-Country Evidence. *Applied Research in Quality of Life*, 1-13.

Nikolaev, B., & Salahodjaev, R. (2016). The role of intelligence in the distribution of national happiness. *Intelligence*, 56, 38-45.

Nikolova, M. (2016). Minding the happiness gap: Political institutions and perceived quality of life in transition. *European journal of political economy*, 45, 129-148.

Ochsen, C., & Welsch, H. (2012). Who benefits from labor market institutions? Evidence from surveys of life satisfaction. *Journal of Economic Psychology*, 33(1), 112-124.

Rodríguez-Pose, A., & Maslauskaite, K. (2012). Can policy make us happier? Individual characteristics, socio-economic factors and life satisfaction in Central and Eastern Europe. *Cambridge Journal of Regions, Economy and Society*, 5(1), 77-96.

Salahodjaev, R. (2021). Tolerance, governance and happiness (in) equality: cross-country evidence. *International Journal of Development Issues*.

Salahodjaev, R., Abdullaeva, B., Tosheva, S., & Isaeva, A. (2020). Female parliamentarians and the distribution of national happiness. *Applied Research in Quality of Life*, 1-15.

Shaw, J. W., Horrace, W. C., & Vogel, R. J. (2005). The determinants of life expectancy: an analysis of the OECD health data. *Southern Economic Journal*, 768-783.

Sede, P. I., & Ohemeng, W. (2015). Socio-economic determinants of life expectancy in Nigeria (1980–2011). *Health economics review*, 5(1), 1-11.

Spruk, R., & Kešeljević, A. (2016). Institutional origins of subjective well-being: Estimating the effects of economic freedom on national happiness. *Journal of happiness studies*, 17(2), 659-712.

Stroup, M. D. (2007). Economic freedom, democracy, and the quality of life. *World Development*, 35(1), 52-66.

Young, F. W. (2001). Structural pluralism and life expectancy in less-developed countries: the role of women's status. *Social Indicators Research*, 55(2), 223-240.

Yu, Z., Bo, W., & Shu, L. (2011, September). The dynamic relationship between satisfaction with local government, family income, and life satisfaction in China: A 6-year perspective. In *2011 International Conference on Management Science & Engineering 18th Annual Conference Proceedings* (pp. 1207-1214). IEEE.

Chapter 5

Globalization and Carbon Emissions

Akram Ishnazarov[*] and Feruza Shamsieva

Tashkent State University of Economics, Uzbekistan

Abstract

This study investigates the relationship between KOF globalization index and carbon dioxide emissions in Belt and Road economies between 1995-2015. We conduct panel cointegration and causality tests and report short- and long-term coefficients of KOF globalization index. Pedroni, Kao and Westerlund cointegration test results reveal long-term cointegrating relationship between the variables. Results of pooled mean group (PMG) regression suggests positive and significant short- and long-term relationship between KOF globalization and CO2 emissions. Error correction term suggests that it will take around two years to reach the half of existing disequilibrium. Dumitrescu and Hurlin panel non-causality test fails to reject the null hypothesis of no causal relationship between KOF globalization and CO2 in selected sample.

Keywords: KOF globalization index, CO^2 emissions

Introduction

Globalization has been rapidly changing human life since the 1990s in economic, social, and political contexts, increasing the well-being of developing and developed nations. Economies pursuing globalization enjoy higher growth rates (Dreher, 2006), especially regarding economic

[*] Corresponding Author's Email: a.ishnazarov77@gmail.com.

In: Economic Growth and Wellbeing
Editor: Raufhon Salahodjaev
ISBN: 978-1-68507-990-1

integration, which creates many opportunities for economic development, promoting free trade and capital flows. Global economic integration affects economies and society in many ways. It promotes business development by increasing competition in national markets once foreign players enter. At the same time, it lowers trade barriers, allowing national companies to expand their sales geography and increase their sales in foreign markets.

Consequently, quality products and services can be improved and followed by price reduction due to harsh competition and technology spread. Improved access to capital markets, information, knowledge, and technology creates an opportunity for quick adjustment to constantly changing economic, social, and political conditions. Moreover, stronger international cooperation enhances how relatively underdeveloped economies may learn from developed ones, adopting best international practices in their development path.

On the other hand, environmental degradation is a big concern worldwide, and with ever-growing aspirations for economic growth, it has become more critical. During the last 60 years, carbon dioxide emissions have increased substantially and reached a record of 36,441 metric tons in 2019[1]. Along with expanding industries, trade, export and tourism development, a number of different environmental and health consequences, including air pollution, smog, and respiratory diseases, are encountered by the population. Moreover, pollutant emissions are responsible for global temperature rise, shifts in precipitation, sea level rises and overall climate change. Such extreme weather conditions consequently disrupt food supply chains, thereby undermining food security. Currently, there are about 7 million deaths caused by air pollution. It is estimated that by 2050, antibiotic resistance to pollutants in drinking water will become the leading cause of death, female and male infertility[2].

Belt and Road economies are of particular interest in this context. Historically, 71 economies, different in socio-economic, political and cultural context, were connected by a caravan road from East Asia to the Mediterranean in the Middle Ages, representing one of the earliest forms of globalization. Nowadays, their commitment to international cooperation is even stronger. The Belt and Road Initiative includes 1/3 of world trade and GDP, and over 60% of the world's population.[3] In particular, China has greatly benefited from globalization since it has been increasing cross-border flows of capital and goods (Wang, 2019) and consequently has become the largest

---

[1] World Bank, Global Carbon Atlas
[2] https://www.un.org/en/climatechange/science/key-findings
[3] https://www.worldbank.org/en/topic/regional-integration/brief/belt-and-road-initiative

exporter in the world. Globalization substantially improved the economy of such a small country like Singapore that face a shortage of natural resources on top of that. The country's success is attributed to export-oriented industrialization and cooperation with multinationals and the private sector (Lai-To, 2000). In 2020, Singapore became the 18th most globalized economy in the world.

At the same time, many Belt and Road economies prioritize economic growth at the expense of the environment. According to Air Quality index, the top 16 most polluted countries globally are Belt and Road economies[4]. Many countries (e.g., Russia, Syria, United Arab Emirates, Saudi Arabia, etc.) are abundant with natural resources such as oil, gas, and coal, which become the main source of their economic prosperity. Lack of environmental policies, rising aspiration for further economic expansion resulting in larger production volumes, greater energy consumption, and rising international trade strengthen the need for policy intervention in preventing environmental shocks.

The remainder of the paper is structured in the following way. Section 2 reviews the previous research on the relationship between globalization and environmental pollution. It also describes the sample and variables. Section 3 discusses methods and empirical results.

Literature Review

To the best of our knowledge, the last decade has been marked by a significant increase in the literature dedicated to the relationship between globalization and environmental degradation. It is interesting to consider the existing empirical evidence on the pollution-globalization interrelations in more detail. These pieces of evidence contain both panel and time-series results.

For instance, the evidence on the globalization-emission association is proposed by Leitão (2014) using the case of Portugal from 1970 to 2010. Surprisingly, the author documents the unidirectional strands from emission level to globalization based on the Granger non-causality procedure. Further, Shahbaz et al. (2015) explore the association between carbon emission and globalization using the data on India between 1970 and 2012. The long-run estimates document that acceleration of globalization results in the growth of environmental pollution. However, authors fail to identify the existence of a

---

[4] https://www.iqair.com/us/world-most-polluted-countries

causal relationship between variables. Furthermore, the estimates of the CO2-globalization relationship in China over the period between 1970 and 2012 proposed by Shahbaz et al. (2017) document the negative impact of the overall index and sub-indicators of globalization on carbon dioxide emission. The VECM framework estimates reveal the existence of short- and long-run cointegrated relationships among variables and prove the EKC model's validity in China over the observed period.

Moreover, the analysis indicates the presence of unidirectional causal nexus running from carbon emission level to globalization. Similarly, Van and Bao (2018) use the data on Vietnam from 1985 to 2015. The results demonstrate the existence of short- and long-run cointegrated relations between carbon emission levels and globalization. The results prove the negative impact of globalization in Vietnam on the level of carbon emission. The other time-series evidence on the globalization-emission nexus is provided by Shahbaz et al. (2018), using the data on Japan over the period from 1970 to 2014. The obtained results show the existence of threshold asymmetric cointegration among variables.

Besides, the authors state that the effect of negative threshold-based shocks in globalization on CO2 emission is more profound than in the case of positive threshold-based shocks. Additionally, the other evidence on the carbon-globalization nexus is provided by Khan et al. (2019) using the sample of Pakistan from 1971 to 2016. The results of the ARDL simulations model document that economic, social, and political globalization and other economic indicators such as energy use, financial development, trade, and FDI stimulate the growth of carbon dioxide emission in both short- and long-run. On the other hand, Salahuddin et al. (2019b) investigate the association between globalization and CO2 emission in the case of South Africa from 1980 to 2017. The ARDL cointegration procedure proves the existence of short- and long-run cointegrated relationships between variables. However, authors fail to identify any causal link between globalization and carbon emission in South Africa within this period.

Similarly, Khan and Ullah (2019) provide the time-series estimates of Pakistan during 1975 and 2014. The results show that globalization and carbon emission are cointegrated in the long run. The findings document that elasticities of several types of globalization, including economic, political, and social globalization, increase environmental degradation by 0.38, 0.19, and 0.11%, respectively. Similar to Shahbaz et al. (2019), authors prove the existence of inverted U-shaped nature of the association between variables. The other time-series analysis proposed by Akadiri et al. (2020) is based on the data on Turkey. The analysis uses the data from 1970 to 2014. The obtained results are contradictory because the cointegration procedure proves that variables are cointegrated. Still, the ARDL fails to identify the statistically significant elasticity between them in both short- and long-run. The causality approach demonstrates the unidirectional nexus from globalization to carbon emission level.

Considering the existing panel evidence on the carbon-globalization nexus, one of the early studies is provided by Leitão (2013) using a sample of selected 18 countries. The results of GMM procedure show that globalization has a positive and statistically significant impact on carbon emission levels. Further, Shabaz et al. (2016) state that globalization negatively affects the carbon emission level in Angola, Cameroon, Congo Republic, Egypt, Kenya, Libya, Tunisia, and Zambia but increases environmental degradation in Ghana, Morocco, South Africa, Sudan, and Tanzania within the period from 1971 to 2012. On the other hand, You and Lv (2018) provide evidence on pollution-globalization association using a panel of 83 economies within a period between 1985 and 2013. According to the results, there are spatial correlations in carbon emission levels across countries. The finding demonstrates that the indirect negative effect of globalization on environmental pollution level is stronger and more statistically significant than positive direct effect. Similarly, Kalayci and Hayaloğlu (2019) examine the effect of globalization and international trade on carbon emissions in NAFTA countries from 1990 to 2015. Similar to the findings provided by Shahbaz et al. (2017), authors prove the validity of EKC hypothesis.

However, the estimates demonstrate the positive association between globalization and environmental degradation expressed by carbon dioxide emission level. Another evidence on the globalization-emission relationship is provided by Shahbaz et al. (2019). Authors apply the EKC hypothesis to prove the existence of non-linear relationship between globalization and carbon emission. The results for 16 high- and middle-income countries out of the whole sample of 87 countries document the validity of the EKC hypothesis, implying that while globalization positively affects the rise of CO_2 emission in the short run, it will lead to a decline in the level of pollution in the long run. Similarly, Zaidi et al. (2019) provide panel evidence of Asia Pacific Economic Cooperation (APEC) countries over the period 1990 and 2016. The results demonstrate that globalization and CO_2 emission are cointegrated. Continuously Updated Bias-Corrected (CUP-BC) and Continuously Updated Fully Modified (CUP-FM) show that globalization has negative elasticity with the level of environmental degradation in the long run.

Moreover, the Granger causality test results indicate the unidirectional strand running from globalization to carbon emission level. One of the recent studies provided by Liu et al. (2020) applies semi-parametric analysis for the sample of G7 countries between 1970 and 2015. The obtained results demonstrate that the carbon-globalization association follows EKC inverted U-shaped nature. On the other hand, the growth of national income positively relates to environmental degradation, while renewable energy consumption has a negative association with carbon emission levels. Further, Wang et al. (2020) provide the estimates of carbon-globalization interrelations in the case of G7 countries over the period from 1996 to 2017. Authors employ the CS-ARDL cointegration procedure and document the existence of cointegrated relationship between indicators. The results demonstrate that globalization increases the level of carbon emission.

Similarly, one of the recent studies on the association between carbon emission and globalization is provided by Alola and Joshua (2020) and documents the mixed results. The authors use the sample of high-, middle-, and low-income countries between 1970 and 2014. The effect of globalization in the short- and long-run is negative and positive respectively but is proved to be significant only in lower-income countries.

The review of existing empirical evidence on the globalization-emission interrelations provide controversial results. The rest of the study is structured as follows: the description of the data, the methodology employed in the current analysis, obtained results and corresponding conclusion with suggested policy recommendations.

Data

This study empirically investigates the relationship between globalization and carbon emissions in Belt and Road economies between 1995-2015. Because several empirical tests and methodologies require strongly balanced data, 59[5]

---

[5] Albania, Armenia, Azerbaijan, Bangladesh, Belarus, Bhutan, Bosnia and Herzegovina, Bulgaria, Cambodia, China, Croatia, Czech Republic, Egypt, Arab Rep., Estonia, Georgia, Greece, Hong Kong SAR, China, Hungary, India, Indonesia, Iran Islamic Rep., Iraq, Israel, Jordan, Kazakhstan, Kenya, Kyrgyz Republic, Lao PDR, Latvia, Lebanon, Lithuania, Malaysia, Maldives, Moldova, Mongolia, Myanmar, Nepal, North Macedonia, Pakistan, Philippines, Poland, Romania, Russian Federation, Saudi Arabia, Serbia, Singapore, Slovak Republic, Slovenia, Sri Lanka, Tajikistan, Tanzania, Thailand, Turkey, Turkmenistan, Ukraine, United Arab Emirates, Uzbekistan, Vietnam, Yemen, Rep.

countries were included in our sample. The final sample contains more than 1,180 observations. Table 1 provides summary statistics.

CO2 Emissions

The dependent variable in our study is carbon emissions, which are measured in per capita terms with the average value in our sample yielding 4.8 metric tons per capita. According to Figure 1, carbon dioxide emissions is increasing between 1995-2015 in Belt and Road countries. In our sample, the largest CO2 emissions are observed in United Arab Emirates (24.93), Saudi Arabia (15.89), Estonia (12.78), Kazakhstan (11.77), Czech Republic (11.64), Russian Federation (10.8), Singapore (10.16), Turkmenistan (10.04), Israel (9.31), and Greece (9.03).

KOF Globalization Index

The main independent variable is globalization. Following Shahbaz et al., (2017), globalization is measured by KOF globalization index, which was initially introduced by Dreher (2006). KOF globalization index is extensively used among researchers as a proxy for globalization (Zerrin et al., 2018; Shahbaz et al., 2019; Gozgor et al., 2020) as it has become the most widespread measure of globalization in academic literature (Potrafke, 2015).

The index is divided into three dimensions according to main globalization channels – economic, political and social. According to Dreher (2006), economic globalization represents long distance flows of goods, capital and services as well as information. Political dimension of globalization can be characterized as policies diffusion, while social globalization stands for ideas and information spreading. The index distinguishes between de facto and de jure measures and their combination forms overall index of globalization (Gygli et al., 2019). In our sample average globalization score yields 58.7 with the maximum value of 86.2. The 10 most globalized countries in our sample are Singapore (81.7), Hungary (81.7), Czech Republic (79.7), Greece (77.5), Estonia (77.0), Slovak Republic (76.0), Malaysia (75.9), Poland (74.3), Israel (74.1) and Slovenia (74.0).

Arkam Ishnazarov and Feruza Shamsieva

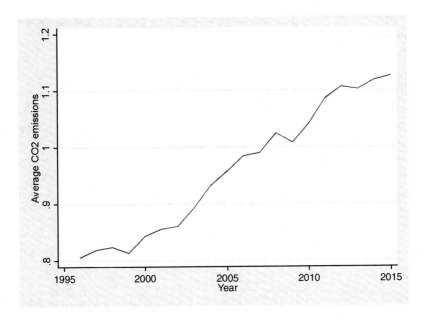

Figure 1. Average carbon emissions.

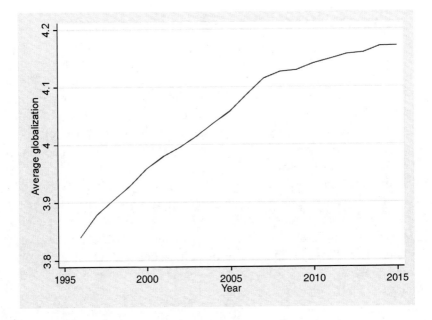

Figure 2. Average globalization.

Table 1. Descriptive statistics

Variable	Indicator	Source	Mean	Std. Dev.	Min	Max
C	CO2 emissions per capita (metric tons)	Global Carbon Atlas	4.795218	4.719053	0.075206	35.6688
G	KOF index of globalization	KOF Swiss Economic Institute	58.69806	14.44437	22.8	86.2
Y	GDP per capita (constant 2010 US$)	WDI	7687.178	10175.74	250	64516.13
RE	Renewable energy consumption (% of total final energy consumption)	WDI	24.67461	27.20092	0.0019716	94.37175

Methods and Results

Model

We model carbon dioxide emission in the following way:

$$C_{i,t} = f(G_{i,t}, Y_{i,t}, RE_{i,t}) \tag{1}$$

where C represents CO_2 emissions per capita, G is KOF index of globalization, Y is GDP per capita, and RE is renewable energy consumption.

As Paramati et al. (2017) suggest, natural log transformation enables all variables to follow the same measurement unit. Variables in logarithmic transformation demonstrate better distributional properties due to decreased data sharpness, helping to avoid autocorrelation and heteroscedasticity, increasing the consistency and efficiency of the model (Zafar et al., 2020).

Thus, we transform all the variables in Eq. 1 into natural logarithm:

$$\ln C_{i,t} = \beta_0 + \beta_1 \ln G_{i,t} + \beta_2 \ln Y_{i,t} + \beta_3 \ln RE_{i,t} \tag{2}$$

where $\ln C_{i,t}$ is natural log of CO_2 emissions per capita, $\ln G_{i,t}$ is natural log of KOF globalization index, $\ln Y_{i,t}$ is natural log of GDP per capita and $\ln RE_{i,t}$ is natural log of renewable energy consumption.

Table 2. Panel unit-root test

Form	Variable	Test		
		IPS	ADF Fisher	PP Fisher
Level	ln CO2	3.3178	154.5802	122.3335
		(0.9995)	(0.0134)	(0.3737)
First-difference	Δ ln CO2	-15.8926*	589.1254*	1037.4684*
		(0.0000)	(0.0000)	(0.0000)
Level	ln KOF	-6.0369*	288.6153*	379.2423*
		(0.0000)	(0.0000)	(0.0000)
First-difference	Δ ln KOF	-13.5528*	343.8555*	709.4029*
		(0.0000)	(0.0000)	(0.0000)
Level	ln Y	8.2984	42.4367	85.2346
		(1.0000)	(1.0000)	(0.9900)
First-difference	Δ ln Y	-15.5942*	492.0966*	1052.2878*
		(0.0000)	(0.0000)	(0.0000)
Level	ln RE	2.9864	82.1054	139.3828
		(0.9986)	(0.9951)	(0.0871)
First-difference	Δ ln RE	-15.9418*	533.9934*	1095.0808*
		(0.0000)	(0.0000)	(0.0000)

* indicates significance at 1% significance level. Figures in parentheses are p-values.

Table 3. Panel cointegration tests results

Test statistic	Score
V-stat	-0.334
Panel rho-stat	-6.534***
Panel PP-stat	-19.82***
Panel ADF-stat	2.651***
Group rho stat	-3.893***
Group PP stat	-23.44***
Group ADF stat	7.929***
Kao's ADF	- 18.1421***
Variance ratio	-4.0682***

Note: ***, ** and * indicate significance at 1%, 5% and 10% levels, respectively.

Cointegration Analysis

Following Salahuddin et al. (2019a), we employ Pedroni's (1999, 2004) one-tailed panel cointegration test for heterogeneous panels to estimate the Eq.1. Pedroni's test examines the null hypothesis of no cointegration using seven test statistics grouped into group-mean statistics and panel statistics. The former averages the results of individual country test statistics and the latter pools the statistics along the within-dimension (Neal, 2014). The null hypothesis is rejected when most test-statistics favor the alternative one. The test allows heterogeneity of the panel in the short- and long-term dynamics and intercepts coefficients. All test statistics follow the normal distribution. We conduct Kao (1999) and Westerlund (2005) panel cointegration tests as a measure of robustness.

Prior to the cointegration test, the order of integration should be investigated. According to Pedroni (1999), some linear combination of variables, which are individually integrated of order one and stationary, may exhibit cointegrating relationship. For this purpose, we employ the IPS panel unit root test introduced by Im et al. (2003). IPS test follows normal Dickey Fuller averaging and is applicable in panel datasets with serial correlation patterns of different orders (Im et al., 2003). The null hypothesis assumes non-stationarity in every individual panel series, while the alternative one states stationarity of at least one panel. To ensure the robustness of the test results, we additionally run the Fisher-type panel unit-root test developed by Maddala and Wu (1999).

We first report panel unit-root test results in Table 2. All variables, except for the KOF globalization index are non-stationary at the level form, yet when integrated of order of one, all variables are stationary. Table 3 provides the result for Pedroni, Kao, and Westerlund's panel cointegration tests. Six out of seven test statistics related to Pedroni's test reject the null hypothesis of no cointegration at a 1% significance level. Kao and Westerlund's test results confirm a cointegrating relationship as well.

Short- and Long-Term Estimates

Once the cointegrating relationship is confirmed, we apply the dynamic Pooled Mean Group (PMG) estimator regression technique proposed by Pesaran et al., (1999) to differentiate between the short- and long-term effects of globalization within the dynamic panel error-correction framework. Formed as reparameterization of the autoregressive distributed lag (ARDL) model, PMG keeps long-term coefficients constant, yet allows heterogeneity in short-term coefficients and error variances across groups. Blackburne and Frank (2007) explain that cointegrated variables are responsive to deviations from long-run equilibrium, thereby implying an error correction model (ECM), where short-term dynamics of the variables are influenced by the deviations from equilibrium. The following equation corresponds to the reparameterization of dynamic panel ARDL into an error correction equation:

$$\Delta y_{it} = \phi_i \left(y_{i,t-1} - \theta_i' X_{it} \right) + \sum_{j=1}^{p-1} \lambda_{i,j}^* \Delta y_{i,t-1} + \sum_{j=0}^{q-1} \delta_{ij}'^* \Delta X_{i,t-j} + \mu_i + \epsilon_{it} \quad (3)$$

where, in our case, y_{it} is CO_2 emissions, x_is are independent variables (KOF, Y and RE), $\lambda_{i,j}^*$ and $\delta_{ij}'^*$ are the short-term coefficients, θ_i' is the long-term coefficient, μ_i group specific effects and ϵ_{it} stochastic error term.

PMG estimates reveal a positive and highly significant long-term relationship between the KOF globalization index and carbon emissions at $p < 0.01$. In the short-term, the effect of globalization is positive and significant at $p < 0.05$. GDP per capita and renewable energy decrease CO2 emissions in the long-term, yet the coefficient of economic growth turns insignificant in the short-term. Our estimates suggest that 27% of the long-term disequilibrium converge before the next time period, yet 73% remain. The short-term error correction term is -0.27, which means that 27% of existing disequilibrium is dissipated before the next time period. In other words, it will take around two years to reach the half of existing disequilibrium.

Table 4. Pesaran's pooled mean group estimator results

Δ ln CO₂ emissions (dependent variable)	Pooled mean group	
Variable	Coefficient	Standard error
Long-term coefficients		
Ln KOF	0.4797*** (0.000)	0.055
ln Y	-0.3932*** (0.000)	0.032
ln RE	-0.3932*** (0.000)	0.023
Error correction term	-0.2718*** (0.000)	0.036
Δ ln KOF	0.3288** (0.026)	0.1479
Δ ln Y	0.1101 (0.250)	0.0956
Δ ln RE	-0.8071*** (0.005)	0.2875
Intercept	-0.9593*** (0.000)	0.1305

Note: ***, ** and * indicate significance at 1%, 5% and 10% levels, respectively. While figures in parentheses are p-values.

Causality Analysis

After the cointegrating relationship is confirmed, we proceed with identifying causality direction since it is important for deriving policy implications. We, therefore, employ panel Dumitrescu and Hurlin's non-causality test for heterogeneous panel data in the presence of cross-sectional dependence introduced by Dumitrescu and Hurlin (2012). The benchmark model is presented below, where $x_{i,t}$ and $y_{i,t}$ are observations of two stationary variables for individual i in period.

$$y_{i,t} = \alpha_i + \sum_{k=1}^{K} \gamma_{ik} y_{i,t-k} + \sum_{k=1}^{K} \beta_{ik} x_{i,t-k} + \varepsilon_{i,t} \qquad (3)$$

The test is based on the individual Wald statistics under the null hypothesis that assumes non-causal relationship and is tested by *z-bar* and *z-bar tilde*. The test is suitable for large and small panels, yet for relatively large number of observations (N) and relatively small time periods (T), Lopez and Weber (2017) suggest drawing empirical conclusions based on *z-bar tilde* statistics.

Table 6 describes the results of panel DH causality test. We first test if KOF globalization index causes CO_2 emissions in our sample. We fail to reject the null hypothesis of non-causal relationship between variables since *z-bar tilde* statistics is higher than critical. Similarly, CO_2 emissions do not Granger-cause globalization in our data. In other words, our results do not reveal any causal relationship between the KOF globalization index and carbon dioxide emissions. Our findings are in line with Salahuddin et al. (2019a), who observed no causality between globalization and CO_2 emissions in Sub-Saharan Africa.

Table 6. DH panel non-causality test

Null hypothesis	Statistic z-bar tilde	Optimal number of lags (AIC)	Lags tested
Δ ln KOF doesn't Granger-cause Δ ln CO2	0.8430	1	1-4
	(0.3992)		
Δ ln CO2 doesn't Granger-cause Δ ln KOF	-0.8770	1	1-4
	(0.3805)		

Note: ***, ** and * indicate significance at 1%, 5% and 10% levels, respectively. While figures in parentheses are p-values.

Conclusion

Over the past three decades, globalization has increased rapidly, interconnecting world economies through trade, tourism, financial and social capital flows. At the same time, the environment has degraded largely and human activity is the main cause. Belt and Road economies represent an interesting example of countries historically committed to increased interstate cooperation, thanks to the Great Silk Road, and on the other hand, great aspiration to economic prosperity at the expense of the environment. Many Belt and Road countries significantly expanded their economies by establishing larger interstate cooperation. Meanwhile, many of them experience environmental issues.

To the best of our knowledge, previous research analyzes the relationship between globalization and CO2 emissions in some separate countries or separate groups of countries of Belt and Road economies (Shahbaz et al., 2017; Khan et al., 2019; Nguyen and Le, 2020; Yuan et al., 2021). Our research is dedicated to globalization-pollution relationship, employing a sample of 59 Belt and Roads economies between 1995-2015.

We employ Pedroni's panel cointegration test and panel Granger causality test. Short- and long-term elasticities are reported with Pooled Mean Group (PMG) estimator. Our findings confirm a significant long-term relationship between globalization and carbon emissions in our sample. PMG estimates suggest that the relationship is positive and significant in short- and long-term. The short-term error correction is 27%, meaning that it will take around two years to reach the half of existing disequilibrium. Moreover, in the long-term, economic development and higher shares of renewable energy negatively 27%, which means that related to carbon emissions. In the short term, however, economic growth enhances pollution.

Our findings may provide some policy suggestions. First, higher interstate cooperation is positively associated with the environmental pollution in Belt and Road countries. Economic growth, which is positively related to CO2 emissions in the short term, has not outweighed negative environmental consequences. This strengthens the need for policymakers to intervene and impose environmental regulations. It also means that Belt and Road economies are still far from using globalization's benefits to improve environmental conditions (Salahuddin et al., 2019a).

On the contrary, economic prosperity is still largely dependent on extensive energy use, and environmental risks are not taken into account. Secondly, since there is no causal relationship between the variables, policies aimed at the reduction of carbon dioxide emissions will not directly harm international cooperation. On the other hand, some measures may even enhance globalization. For instance, green energy investment projects may be implemented in tight cooperation with other countries, attracting significant foreign capital inflows.

References

Akadiri, S., Alola, A. A., Olasehinde-Williams, G., & Etokakpan, M. U. (2020). The role of electricity consumption, globalization and economic growth in carbon dioxide emissions and its implications for environmental sustainability targets. *Science of The Total Environment*, *708*, 134653.

Alola, A. A., & Joshua, U. (2020). Carbon emission effect of energy transition and globalization: inference from the low-, lower middle-, upper middle-, and high-income economies. *Environmental Science and Pollution Research*, *27*(30), 38276-38286.

Blackburne III, E. F., & Frank, M. W. (2007). Estimation of nonstationary heterogeneous panels. *The Stata Journal*, *7*(2), 197-208.

Dreher, A. (2006). Does globalization affect growth? Evidence from a new index of globalization. *Applied economics*, *38*(10), 1091-1110.

Dumitrescu, E. I., & Hurlin, C. (2012). Testing for Granger non-causality in heterogeneous panels. *Economic modelling*, 29(4), 1450-1460.

Gozgor, G., Mahalik, M. K., Demir, E., & Padhan, H. (2020). The impact of economic globalization on renewable energy in the OECD countries. *Energy Policy*, *139*, 111365.

Gygli, S., Haelg, F., Potrafke, N., & Sturm, J. E. (2019). The KOF globalisation index–revisited. *The Review of International Organizations*, *14*(3), 543-574.

Im, K. S., M. H. Pesaran, and Y. Shin. (2003). Testing for unit roots in heterogeneous panels. *Journal of Econometrics*, 115: 53-74.

Kalayci, C. (2019). The impact of economic globalization on CO2 emissions: the case of NAFTA countries. *International Journal of Energy Economics and Policy*, 9(1), 356.

Kao, C. (1999). Spurious regression and residual-based tests for cointegration in panel data. *Journal of Econometrics*, *90*, 1-44.

Khan, D., & Ullah, A. (2019). Testing the relationship between globalization and carbon dioxide emissions in Pakistan: does environmental Kuznets curve exist? *Environmental Science and Pollution Research*, *26*(15), 15194-15208.

Khan, M. K., Teng, J. Z., Khan, M. I., & Khan, M. O. (2019). Impact of globalization, economic factors and energy consumption on CO2 emissions in Pakistan. *Science of the total environment*, *688*, 424-436.

Lai-To, L. (2000). Singapore's globalization strategy. *East Asia*, *18*(2), 36-49.

Leitão, N. C. (2013). Carbon dioxide emissions, urbanization and globalization: a dynamic panel data. *Economic Research Guardian*, 22-32.

Leitão, N. C. (2014). Economic growth, carbon dioxide emissions, renewable energy and globalization. *International Journal of Energy Economics and Policy*, *3*, 391-399.

Liu, M., Ren, X., Cheng, C., & Wang, Z. (2020). The role of globalization in CO2 emissions: a semi-parametric panel data analysis for G7. *Science of the Total Environment*, *718*, 137379.

Lopez, L., & Weber, S. (2017). Testing for Granger causality in panel data. *The Stata Journal*, *17*(4), 972-984.

Maddala, G. S., & Wu, S. (1999). A comparative study of unit root tests with panel data and a new simple test. *Oxford Bulletin of Economics and statistics*, *61*(S1), 631-652.

Neal, T., (2014). Panel cointegration analysis with xtpedroni. *The Stata Journal*, *14*(3), 684-692.

Nguyen, T., & Le, Q. (2020). Impact of globalization on CO2 emissions in Vietnam: An autoregressive distributed lag approach. *Decision Science Letters*, *9*(2), 257-270.

Paramati, S. R., Shahbaz, M., & Alam, M. S. (2017). Does tourism degrade environmental quality? A comparative study of Eastern and Western European Union. *Transportation Research Part D: Transport and Environment*, *50*, 1-13.

Pedroni, P. (1999). Critical values for cointegration tests in heterogeneous panels with multiple regressors. *Oxford Bulletin of Economics and Statistics*, *61*, 653-670.

Pedroni, P. (2001). Fully modified OLS for heterogeneous cointegrated panels in Nonstationary panels, panel cointegration, and dynamic panels. Emerald Group Publishing Limited.

Pedroni, P. (2004). Panel cointegration: asymptotic and finite sample properties of pooled time series tests with an application to the PPP hypothesis. *Econometric theory*, 597-625.

Potrafke, N. (2015). The evidence on globalisation. *The World Economy*, *38*(3), 509-552.

Salahuddin, M., Ali, M. I., Vink, N., & Gow, J. (2019a). The effects of urbanization and globalization on CO2 emissions: evidence from the Sub-Saharan Africa (SSA) countries. *Environmental Science and Pollution Research*, *26*(3), 2699-2709.

Salahuddin, M., Gow, J., Ali, M. I., Hossain, M. R., Al-Azami, K. S., Akbar, D., & Gedikli, A. (2019b). Urbanization-globalization-CO2 emissions nexus revisited: empirical evidence from South Africa. *Heliyon*, *5*(6), e01974.

Shahbaz, M., Khan, S., Ali, A., & Bhattacharya, M. (2017). The impact of globalization on CO2 emissions in China. *The Singapore Economic Review*, *62*(04), 929-957.

Shahbaz, M., Mahalik, M. K., Shahzad, S. J. H., & Hammoudeh, S. (2019). Testing the globalization-driven carbon emissions hypothesis: international evidence. *International Economics*, *158*, 25-38.

Shahbaz, M., Mallick, H., Mahalik, M. K., & Loganathan, N. (2015). Does globalization impede environmental quality in India? *Ecological Indicators*, *52*, 379-393.

Shahbaz, M., Shahzad, S. J. H., & Mahalik, M. K. (2018). Is globalization detrimental to CO2 emissions in Japan? New threshold analysis. *Environmental Modeling & Assessment*, *23*(5), 557-568.

Shahbaz, M., Solarin, S. A., & Ozturk, I. (2016). Environmental Kuznets curve hypothesis and the role of globalization in selected African countries. *Ecological Indicators*, *67*, 623-636.

Van, D. T. B., & Bao, H. H. G. (2018). The role of globalization on CO2 emission in Vietnam incorporating industrialization, urbanization, GDP per capita and energy use. *International Journal of Energy Economics and Policy*, *8*(6), 275.

Wang, H. (2019). China and globalization: 40 years of Reform and Opening-up and globalization 4.0. *Journal of Chinese Economic and Business Studies, 17*(3), 215-220.

Wang, L., Vo, X. V., Shahbaz, M., & Ak, A. (2020). Globalization and carbon emissions: Is there any role of agriculture value-added, financial development, and natural resource rent in the aftermath of COP21?. *Journal of Environmental Management, 268*, 110712.

Westerlund, J. (2005). New simple tests for panel cointegration. *Econometric Reviews, 24*(3), 297-316.

You, W., & Lv, Z. (2018). Spillover effects of economic globalization on CO2 emissions: a spatial panel approach. *Energy Economics, 73*, 248-257.

Yuan, J., Wu, Y., Jing, W., Liu, J., Du, M., Wang, Y., & Liu, M. (2021). Non-linear correlation between daily new cases of COVID-19 and meteorological factors in 127 countries. *Environmental Research, 193*, 110521.

Zafar, M. W., Shahbaz, M., Sinha, A., Sengupta, T., & Qin, Q. (2020). How renewable energy consumption contribute to environmental quality? The role of education in OECD countries. *Journal of Cleaner Production*, 122149.

Zaidi, S. A. H., Zafar, M. W., Shahbaz, M., & Hou, F. (2019). Dynamic linkages between globalization, financial development and carbon emissions: Evidence from Asia Pacific Economic Cooperation countries. *Journal of Cleaner Production, 228*, 533-543.

Zerrin, K., & Dumrul, Y. (2018). The Impact of Globalization on Economic Growth: Empirical Evidence from the Turkey. *International Journal of Economics and Financial Issues, 8*(5), 115.

Chapter 6

Carbon Emission, Tourism and Renewable Energy

Zebo Kuldasheva[1,*] and Anastas Khachaturov[2,†]

[1]Tashkent State University of Economics, Tashkent, Uzbekistan
[2]ERGO Analytics, Tashkent, Uzbekistan

Abstract

Global climate change over the past 50 years is mainly associated with human activities. Carbon dioxide emission is a major contributor to the deterioration of environmental sustainability. The aim of the current study is to investigate the long-run association among CO_2 emission level, tourism development and renewable energy, as well as validity of Environmental Kuznets Curve (EKC). The study uses the sample of 42 countries of Belt and Road Initiative from 1995 to 2015. The investigation applies Pedroni (1999), Kao (1999) and Westerlund cointegration procedures, Fully Modified Ordinary Least Squares (FMOLS) approach and Dumitrescu and Hurlin (2012) Granger non-causality procedure. General outcomes of the study reveal the existence of long-run cointegration among variables. The tourism development is found to be a positive contributor to the level of carbon emission, while renewable is negatively associated with CO_2 in the long-run. The long-run estimates do not provide evidence on the validity of EKC in the selected countries. Further the results of Granger causality procedure show the uni-directional strand from CO_2 emission to renewable energy and bi-directional nexus between carbon emission and the level of tourism development.

---

* Corresponding Author's Email: kuldashevazebo@gmail.com.
† Corresponding Author's Email: Anastas1@ergorc.com.

In: Economic Growth and Wellbeing
Editor: Raufhon Salahodjaev
ISBN: 978-1-68507-990-1

Introduction

Global climate change remains one of the most serious challenges that humanity faces. The problem of climate change has intensified over the past decade. In 2019, the World Meteorological Organization reported that the past 10 years were the hottest on record within the past 140 years[1]. Also noteworthy is the fact that the first instance of climate change recording coincides with the height of the Second Industrial Revolution, which is notable in part because of the large-scale use of fossil energy sources. The accelerated urbanization and industrialization that the world has faced since that time is associated with the ever-increasing consumption of energy, the main source of which being fossil fuels. The main reason for the rapid climate change over the past 50 years is the increase in carbon dioxide emissions caused by human activities (Anderson et al., 2016; Owusu and Asumadu-Sarkodie, 2016). World GDP during the last 30 years increased by almost 4 times (from $22.63 trillion in 1990 till $87.735 trillion in 2020), while over the past decade, growth amounted to more than $20 trillion.[2] At the same time, the corresponding growth of CO_2 emission during the same period was approximately 14 billion tons.[3]

Tourism remains a significant contributor to economic development (Leitão and Lorente, 2020). Prior to the COVID-19 pandemic, tourism revenues accounted for about 29% of global service export and 7% of total global export of goods and services.[4] However, its impact is rarely studied in the context of environmental sustainability (Solarin, 2014). The exact relationship between tourism and environmental degradation through a rapid increase in the amount of carbon emissions is unclear Some of the existing theoretical and empirical evidence states that the amount of tourism activity can be dampened by undesirable climate conditions, while a particular country's environmental sustainability stimulates the touristic attractiveness of that area (Amelung et al. 2007). At the same time, tourism is associated with an increased amount of carbon emission. Tourism is one of the most

---

[1] WMO Provisional Statement on the State of the Global Climate in 2019 https://library. wmo.int/index.php?lvl=notice_display&id=21626#.YIFowZAzY2w.

[2] https://data.worldbank.org/indicator/NY.GDP.MKTP.KD.ZG.

[3] Global Carbon Project. (2020). Supplemental data of Global Carbon Budget 2020 (Version 1.0) [Data set]. Global Carbon Project. https://doi.org/10.18160/gcp-2020.

[4] https://www.unwto.org/global/press-release/2019-06-06/exports-international-tourism-hit-usd -17-trillion#:~:text=Strong%20growth%20in%20outbound%20travel,exports%20of%20 goods%20and%20services.

energy-intensive sectors due to its strong interconnection with transportation, hospitality and entertainment (Katircioglu, 2014b).

On the other hand, though the Paris Agreement Conference of Parties (COP) announced the end of the era of fossil energy sources; for most countries, these fuels remain the basis of energy security, especially for many developing countries. Thus, the increasing push towards renewables in energy sectors is a pressing challenge for them. As of the first quarter of 2020, the share of renewables in global electricity generation in the was 28%.[5] The evidence reported on the association between carbon emission and share of renewables in energy generation provide contradictory results. The statistically significant short and long run association between CO_2 emissions and renewable energy is proven by a number of previous studies (Sadorsky, 2009; Shafiei and Salim, 2014; Zoundi, 2017). Some of these existing works document the stimulation effect of environmental degradation on the development of renewable energy, which further contributes to the reduction of carbon dioxide emission (Dogan and Seker, 2016). Despite that, other investigations note unidirectional causation only; either from renewable energy to CO_2 (Baloch et al., 2019), or from carbon emission to renewable energy (Menyah and Wolde-Rufael, 2010).

The aim of the current research being conducted is to fill the gap in existing literature on the relationships between carbon-tourism and carbon-renewable energy, considering the possible existence of Environmental Kuznets Curves in the case of countries of the Belt and Road Initiative (BRI hereafter) from 1995 to 2015. The main purposes for the creation of the BRI were to strengthen the international integration of the participating countries, their joint development and the achievement of common interests. The rapid development of the BRI countries and the growth of their GDP was also associated with the depletion of their resource potential and a concomitant decline in the quality of the environment (Hussain et al., 2020). The BRI countries play a significant role in global energy and resource sustainability. These economies account for 58.54% of crude oil (billion barrels), 53.82% of natural gas reserves and 74.69% of coal production.[6] On the other hand, BRI countries contribute to 23.52% of world GDP, while the percentage of the world's population living in these countries is 54.63%. These figures indicate a high level of energy consumption, resulting in about 9816.77 metric tonnes of carbon dioxide emissions in 2014.

---

[5] https://www.iea.org/reports/global-energy-review-2020/renewables.
[6] Statistical Review of World Energy, 2020 | 69th edition.

The study is structured as follows: a brief review of existing empirical literature on carbon-renewable energy and carbon-tourism interrelations; the description of the employed model and econometric methodology; the description of the results and a brief discussion of the findings on the basis of existing evidences; and finally, the study provides the conclusion and policy implications based on the obtained results.

Literature Review

The role of renewable energy in order to achieve a sustainable and clean environment is a well debated topic in recent years. Most studies have analyzed factors affecting energy consumption; likewise, economic growth, trade, GDP, urbanization and population growth were also considered. However, the research on tourism's CO_2 emissions still contains some shortcomings.

This chapter presents reviews of the most relevant literature to describe both the relationship between tourism and carbon emissions, and renewable energy as a solution of environmental degradation.

Tourism and CO_2 Emissions

Tourism is the main driver of economy in tourism-oriented countries, as it promotes the inflow of income, employment and foreign exchange. On the other hand, tourism developments are the main cause of global warming and climate change in most visited countries (Koçak et al., 2020). Tourism activities mainly depend on fossil fuels, as the passengers prefer to travel by airplane rather than other types of transportation, thus increasing global CO_2 emissions (Gössling et al., 2015). Another important factor on environmental pollution is land use due to tourism investments, which causes decreases in forest areas (Bilgili et al., 2017). There is always high demand in the consumption of food in touristic destinations and it requires significant amounts of energy, means more emissions are generated (Gössling et al., 2011). The construction of tourism facilities can also produce massive amounts of carbon emissions even before they open their doors to tourists (Shakouri et al., 2017). Moreover, many touristic accommodations include heating and air conditioning to keep guest rooms at a pleasant temperature in hot or cold climates. Emissions from lodgings tend to be highest in resorts and hotels that offer modern services, while smaller lodgings such as homestays and guest houses have lower emissions for the most part (Sustainable Travel, 2020).

On the other hand, several publications have stated that well-managed tourism may help to protect the environment by implementing ecologically friendly technologies and transportation. Utilization of rail transport can reduce carbon emissions by contributing less to fuel consumption (Paramati et al., 2018). A number of researchers have pointed to the fact that sustainable tourism regulations may improve environmental awareness and that investing in renewable energy sources can reduce environmental degradation (D'Alessandro, 2016; Paramati et al., 2017). Implementing electric vehicles in tourism-oriented countries would significantly reduce the CO_2 emissions, as well as being another attraction for tourists (Sustainable Travel, 2020). According to Paramati et al., (2018), investments in the tourism sphere would allow the industry to grow further by ensuring sustainable tourism development. In general, regulating environmental policies and applying eco-friendly tourism strategies are mostly cited by authors as a path to more environmentally sustainable travel.

The empirical studies below have been divided into country specific and multi-country research regarding the tourism and CO_2 emissions nexus.

Country-Specific Studies on Tourism-CO_2 Emissions

Country-specific research on the tourism-CO_2 nexus investigate the impact of tourism on CO_2 emissions in the context of energy consumption. A recent study by Khanal et al., (2021) examined the link between tourism and energy consumption in the case of Australia over the last four decades (1976-2018). The study aimed to investigate the long-term cointegrating relationship between international tourist arrivals and primary energy consumption in Australia. In the methodology section, the researchers applied Augmented Dickey-Fuller, Phillips-Perron, Autoregressive distributed lag (ARDL) bound tests, Johansen and Juselius, Bayer-Hanck cointegration tests using data from the Australian Bureau of Statistics, BP Statistical Review, and the World Development Indicators. According to the results, tourist arrivals and financial development have a significant long-term cointegrating relationship with energy consumption.

In the case of one of biggest tourist destinations in the world, China, Zhang and Zhang (2021) explored the linkage between tourism, energy consumption and CO_2 emissions for 30 Chinese provinces from 2000 to 2017. The study applied the vector error correction model (VECM) Granger causality approach to investigate the short-run and long-run causal relationships. The results of the research indicate that tourism promotes economic growth and increases CO_2 emissions, respectively. More precisely, higher energy consumption results in higher CO_2 emissions, economic growth, and tourism development. Based on the findings, key policy recommendations were given in order to develop more sustainable tourism in China.

In another study, Katircioglu et al., (2014) analyzed the long-term equilibrium relationship between international tourism, energy consumption, and carbon dioxide emissions in Cyprus. This small island attracts more than 2 million international tourists every year. Through Granger causality tests, major findings indicated that international tourism is a catalyst for energy consumption and for an increase in the level of carbon dioxide emissions in Cyprus. The recommendations based on the study highly encourage the government of Cypriot to adopt measurements for environmental protection.

Eyuboglu and Uzar (2020) analyzed the links between CO_2 emissions, tourist arrivals, and energy consumption for the period 1960 to 2014 in Turkey. The study mainly focused on analyzing the long-term relationships among variables by applying three cointegration tests: Bayer and Hanck, Fourier ADL and ARDL. According to the results, tourism, growth, and energy consumption effect CO_2 positively both in the long and short-term. VECM causality results prove that the main causes of CO_2 emissions are tourism, economic growth, and energy consumption. Additionally, the development of tourism results in higher CO_2 emissions, economic growth, and energy consumption in the long-term. The findings suggest that the tourists should pay more attention to the environmental quality of the country they are travelling to.

In the case of the USA, Raza et al.,(2017) investigated the empirical influence of tourism development on environmental degradation in a high tourist arrival economy for the period of 1996 to 2015, using the wavelet transform framework. The findings imply that there is a positive and significant relationship between tourism development and CO_2 emission in short, medium and long run in the United States. In the case of Malaysia, Solarin (2014) studied the determinants of carbon dioxide emission with special emphasis on tourism development in Malaysia for the period of 1972 to 2010. Cointegration and Granger causality tests were applied to determine the nexus among these variables: GDP, energy consumption, financial development, and urbanization. The findings show long-run correlations between the variables as well as a positive unidirectional long-run causation, which means tourist arrivals are active contributors to pollution. Based on these findings, Malaysian lawmakers should immediately implement policy regulations in order to mitigate the CO_2 emissions and allow for sustainable tourism.

Following similar methods, Sghaier et al., (2019) investigated the impact of tourism development, energy consumption and environmental quality in three African countries: Tunisia, Egypt and Morocco. The study applied an autoregressive distributed lag model to analyze data in the long and short-term nexus among the variables for the period 1980–2014. According to their findings, there is no significant relationship between tourism arrivals and CO_2 emissions in Morocco. On the other hand, tourist arrivals have a decreasing effect on CO_2 emissions in Egypt but have a boosting effect in Tunisia. D'Alessandro (2016) analyzed the new model for green-tourism in the case of Campania region in Italy. The study mainly focuses on region's rural tourism, environmental and cultural assets of the landscape and green building as a solution to a sustainable and clean environment.

Multi Country-Specific Studies on Tourism-CO_2 Emissions

Multi country-specific studies generally investigate the relationship between tourism and CO_2 emissions using panel data techniques to suggest common tourism policies. Dogan and Aslan (2017) explored the relationship between CO_2 emissions, energy consumption and tourism in the EU countries over the period 1995–2011 by using heterogeneous panel estimation techniques with cross-sectional dependence. Their findings show that tourism developments have a reducing effect on carbon emissions. Another study by Paramati et al., (2018) investigated the effect of tourism investments on tourism development and CO_2 emissions in 28 EU nations from 1990 to 2013. The findings reveal that investment in tourism has a significant positive and negative impact on tourism development and CO_2 emissions, respectively. Moreover, tourism investments not only increase tourism revenue but also reduce CO_2 emissions. According to these findings, the authors recommend the delegates of the United Nations to implement more effective policies for tourism investments, as this is the productive way to ensure sustainable tourism development across the member countries.

A recent article by Balsalobre-Lorente and Leitão (2020) studied the role of renewable energy, trade, carbon dioxide emissions and international tourism on economic growth in EU-28, considering panel data for the period 1995–2014. The evidence was derived by using panel fully modified least squares (FMOLS), panel dynamic least squares (DOLS) and fixed effects (FE) as estimation techniques. According to the econometric findings, renewable energy significantly improves environmental quality; however, economic growth contributes to heightened CO_2 emissions, which is directly correlated with climate change. Following the same model and methods, Basarir and Cakir (2015) analyzed the causal interactions between CO_2 emissions, financial development, energy, and tourism in Turkey and four European Countries for the period of 1995 to 2010. According to the findings of the study, a 1% increase in energy consumption will raise carbon dioxide emissions by 3.2% and a 1% increase in financial development will decrease carbon dioxide emissions by 0.11%. Moreover, there is a bi-directional causal relationship between CO_2 emissions, financial development, and energy and tourist arrivals.

A panel study of OECD countries was conducted by Dogan et al., (2017) to investigate the impacts of energy consumption, real GDP, tourism and trade on CO_2 emissions by accounting for cross-sectional dependence. The aim of the research was to analyze the long-run dynamic relationship between CO_2 emissions, energy consumption, GDP and tourism through applying Environmental Kuznets Curve (EKC) model, second-generation unit root tests, cointegration test and the Granger causality test. The dynamic ordinary least squares (DOLS) estimation technique indicates that energy consumption and tourism contribute to the levels of gas emissions, while increases in trade lead to environmental improvements. Based on the research, the leaders of OECD countries are recommended to invest in improving energy efficiency in order to regulate necessary environmental protection policies for tourism sectors.

Because of the lack of econometric studies in the United States of America, Ben Jebli et al., (2019) analyzed the dynamic linkage between renewable energy, tourism, CO_2 emissions, economic growth, foreign direct investment, and trade for a panel of 22 Central and South American countries, spanning the period 1995–2010. The main findings from Granger causality tests demonstrate unidirectional causalities running between both renewable energy to CO_2 emissions and economic growth to renewable energy and tourism, respectively. Long-run estimates prove that tourism, renewable energy, and FDI contribute to the reduction of emissions, while trade and economic growth lead to higher carbon emissions. The study strongly suggests encouraging green tourism in order to combat climate change. In a similar vein of research, Shakouri et al., (2017) examined the influence of tourism and economic growth on CO_2 emissions using panel data of selected Asia-Pacific countries over the period 1995–2013. The authors mainly analyzed the long-run relationship between economic growth, tourism, energy consumption, and CO_2 emissions through testing the Environmental Kuznets Curve hypothesis. The findings reveal that arrivals of tourists have positive effects on carbon dioxide emission levels in the long-run. Moreover, according to the Granger causality test, there is a unidirectional causality from energy consumption to tourism arrivals and a unidirectional causality from CO_2 emissions to tourism arrivals, respectively.

From a sample of Mediterranean countries, Balli et al., (2019) explored the impact of tourism on economic growth considering CO_2 emissions, utilizing panel data technique for the period of 1995–2014. Countries around the Mediterranean Sea are sought after destinations for millions of tourists every year and tourism is a rapidly growing industry in the region. According to the empirical results, tourism expansion improves the economic performance in Egypt, Italy and Spain; however, tourism developments increase the CO_2 emissions in the panel of all Mediterranean countries. The study suggests that policy makers and the tourism industry should collaborate and implement balanced sustainable tourism without harming the environment and touristic attractions.

Finally, comparisons between developed and developing countries were studied by Paramati et al., (2017) to examine the effects of tourism on economic growth and CO_2 emissions. The empirical analysis was carried out separately on 26 developed and 18 developing economies with annual data from 1995 to 2012 by using robust panel econometric techniques and environmental Kuznets curve (EKC) hypothesis. According to the findings, tourism has significant positive impacts on economic growth for both developed and developing economies, though tourism is expected to increase CO_2 emissions in both countries, respectively. Moreover, EKC results suggest that, after reaching a threshold point, the impact of tourism on CO_2 emissions will significantly reduce in developed economies. The study concluded by highlighting necessary policy recommendations for leaders to implement so that that both developed and developing economies can benefit from the positive economic impacts of tourism.

Renewable Energy and CO_2 Emissions

The influence of renewable energy on environmental quality has emerged as a key issue in contemporary energy economic research. Over the past ten years, several studies have investigated the importance of renewable energy and its impact on reducing CO_2 emissions in a sample of different countries. Despite the fact that the literature in this field is dense, the goal of this section is not to review the previous research, but highlight their main conclusions.

For example, a recent study by Saidi and Omri (2020) examined the short and long-run impact of renewable energy consumption on CO_2 emissions in the case of 15 OECD countries from 1990 to 2018. The results of the Fully Modified OLS (FMOLS) show that investment in renewable energy reduces CO_2 emissions in Belgium, Canada, France, Germany, Sweden, UK, US, Japan, Switzerland, Finland, and the Czech Republic; however, it increases CO_2 emissions in the Netherlands and South Korea. Results based on the vector error correction model approach (VECM) method show that renewable energy reduces CO_2 emissions in the long-term. Wolde-rufael and Weldemeskel (2020) investigated the nexus between environmental policy stringency and CO_2 emissions in the case of BRIICTS countries over the period of 1993-2014 using a Panel Pooled Mean Group Autoregressive Distributive Lag (PMG-ARDL) estimator. The findings revealed that renewable energy negatively relates to CO_2 emissions while implementing strict environmental policies after a certain period of time, leading to improvement in environmental quality. The study recommends strengthening environmental policies and promoting the usage of renewable energies for the sake of having a sustainable environment in BRIICTS countries.

In another study by Aydoğan and Vardar (2019) evaluated the role of renewable energy, economic growth and CO_2 emissions and investigated the existence of the Environmental Kuznets Curve (EKC) hypothesis for a panel of E7 countries spanning the period 1990-2014. According to the results, there is a positive relationship between CO_2 emissions and economic growth, while there is also a negative relationship found between CO_2 emissions and renewable energy consumption. It is highly recommended for leaders to increase the share of renewable energy for the sake of economic growth and simultaneously reduce dependency on non-renewable energy consumption in the case of 7E countries. Evidence from developing countries was analyzed by Akram et al., (2020) to examine the heterogeneous effects of energy efficiency and renewable energy on carbon emissions within the context of an environment Kuznets curve (EKC) spanning the period 1990-2014. Panel ordinary least squares and fixed-effect panel quantile regression (PQR) were used to complete the study. The results verified that energy efficiency and renewable energy contribute to reducing carbon emissions in 66 developing countries.

Ikram et al., (2020) investigated the nexus between renewable energy consumption, agriculture and CO_2 emissions in SAARC countries using multiple models covering the years 2000 to 2014. Based on the main findings, India has the highest CO_2 emissions of the countries included. Moreover, in Grey TOPSIS analysis, renewable energy consumption ranked as a top contributor in the reduction of CO_2 emissions. The results of the study have direct implications for policy and decision makers regarding the sustainable development goals (SDGs). Governments of the SAARC countries should target achieving SDGs-2030 agenda with the help of mutual cooperation, support and assistance. It is obvious from the findings that excessive usage of natural resources can affect the environment. A study by Danish et al., (2019) investigated the effect of natural resources, renewable energy and economic development on CO_2 emissions in five BRICS countries for the period of 1990-2015, applying an augmented mean group (AMG) panel algorithm. Based on the findings, natural resources have an insignificant impact on CO_2 emissions in Brazil, China and India. Moreover, a large number of natural resources help to mitigate pollution problems in Russia. Furthermore, renewable energy sources are the primary contributor to the mitigation of environmental deterioration in BRICS nations other than South Africa.

A panel study of European countries was conducted by Shahnazi and Dehghan Shabani (2021) in order to observe the effects of renewable energy and economic freedom on CO_2 emissions in the framework of EKC spanning the period 2000-2017, using a spatial dynamic panel data model. Based on the findings, renewable energy consumption has a negative impact on CO_2 emissions and there is a U-shaped relationship between economic freedom and CO_2 emissions. Another study by Bekun et al., (2019) investigated the long-run and causal interaction between renewable energy consumption, nonrenewable energy consumption, economic growth and CO_2 emissions for selected EU-16 countries over the period of 1996-2014. The results of PMG-ARDL suggests that nonrenewable energy consumption and economic growth increase the CO_2 emissions respectively, while renewable energy reduces it. Effective policy recommendation is given especially in attaining the Sustainable Development Goals.

A recent study by Huang et al. (2021) explored the link between renewable energy and CO_2 emissions in a sample of major renewable energy-consuming countries spanning the period of 2000-2015. The study's main contribution is to answer the issue of whether a significant transition to renewable energy consumption would result in decreased CO_2 emissions. The empirical results of the two-step generalized method of moments (GMM) estimator revealed that renewable energy had a negative influence on CO_2 emissions. Based on the findings, a one-percentage-point increase in renewable energy results in a 0.5-percentage-point reduction in CO_2 emissions. In the case of Sub-Saharan African countries, Adams and Nsiah (2019) studied the nexus between renewable energy and CO_2 emissions for 28 SSA countries using panel cointegration techniques over the period of 1980-2014. Fully Modified OLS and GMM estimation techniques revealed that both renewable and nonrenewable energy increase the CO_2 emissions in the long run but nonrenewable energy has a significant positive effect in the short run. Moreover, it is evidenced that economic growth and urbanization are the main contributors of environmental degradation.

Data and Methodology

This study uses the annual data from 42 countries of Belt and Road Initiative (namely Albania, Armenia, Azerbaijan, Bangladesh, Bulgaria, Belarus, China, Czech Republic, Egypt, Arab Rep., Estonia, Greece, Croatia, Hungary, Indonesia, India, Iran, Islamic Rep., Israel, Jordan, Kazakhstan, Kenya, Kyrgyz Republic, Lao PDR, Lebanon, Sri Lanka, Lithuania, Latvia, Moldova, North Macedonia, Malaysia, Nepal, Pakistan, Philippines, Poland, Romania, Russian Federation, Singapore, Slovak Republic, Slovenia, Thailand, Turkey, Tanzania, Ukraine) from 1995 to 2015. The empirical analysis employs the modified version of the model proposed by Jebli et al. (2016) which accounts for EKC. The general form of the empirical model is presented as follows:

$$\ln CO2_{i,t} = \beta_i + \beta_1 lnRE_{i,t} + \beta_2 lnTOU_{i,t} + \beta_3 lnGDP_{i,t} + \beta_4 lnSQGDP_{i,t} + \beta_5 lnTR_{i,t} + \beta_6 lnFDI_{i,t} + e_{i,t} \tag{1}$$

where lnCO2, lnRE, lnTOU, lnGDP, lnSQGDP, lnTR, lnFDI are logarithmic forms of carbon emission, renewable energy, tourism development, GDP per capita, squared GDP per capita, trade, and foreign direct investment, $i=1...N$ denotes a particular panel, $t=1...T$ represents a year, and $e_{i,t}$ is the error term.

In order to make the data normally distributed and increase the validity of the results, we use logarithmic transformation of the variables included in the model. The descriptive statistics of the data is shown in Table 1.

Table 1. Summary statistics

Variable	Indicator	Source	Mean	Std. Dev.	Min.	Max.	Obs.
CO_2	Carbon emission level (metric tons per capita)	World Bank (2020)	4.715	3.801	0.075	18.141	840
Renewable Energy	Renewable electricity output (% of total electricity output)	World Bank (2020)	26.020	29.276	0.045	100	840
Tourism	International Tourism, Receipts (Current US$) per capita	World Bank (2020)	324.531	508.854	0.281	3561.849	840
GDP	GDP per capita, PPP (current international $)	World Bank (2020)	14890.11	12483.6	1317.56	89366.300	840
FDI	Foreign Direct Investment, Net Inflows (% Of GDP)	World Bank (2020)	4.400	5.741	-15.839	55.076	840
Trade	Trade (% Of GDP)	World Bank (2020)	90.517	57.728	21.930	437.327	

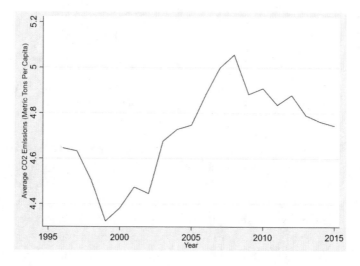

Figure 1. Average CO_2 emission.

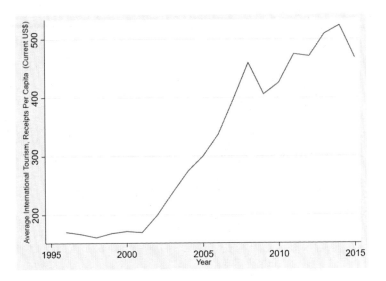

Figure 2. Average tourism receipts per capita.

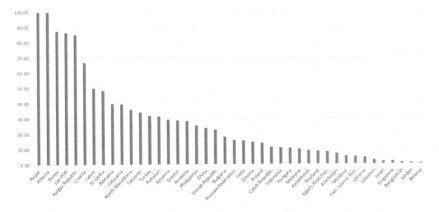

Figure 3. The share of renewable energy in total final energy consumption (%).

The endogenous variable is the level of the carbon emission level which is expressed in metric tons per capita and includes the carbon dioxide emitted during the processing of combustible fuels, including liquid, solid and gaseous, as well as in the production of cement. The main regressors are represented by the share of renewable energy and tourism development. The renewable energy is the share of renewables in total electricity output, while tourism development as expressed by the international tourism receipts are expenditures by international inbound visitors, which includes prepayments for goods and services in the country of destination and transportation costs paid to national carriers. The model contains the set of control variables as well, which includes GDP per capita expressed in current international dollars, converted by purchasing power parity (PPP) conversion factor and squared form of GDP, which accounts for an Environmental Kuznets Curve. Further, the share of net inflow of Foreign Direct Investments in national GDP and trade expressed as the share of sum of exports and imports of goods and services in GDP are also included in the model. It is of interest to trace the dynamics of the selected variables through the observed time path. The second half of the 1990s is marked by a noticeable drop in the level of carbon dioxide emissions. However, after 1999, a rapid increase in emissions began, which continued until the start of the 2008 Global Financial Crisis. The emissions trend then changed to negative again. On the other hand, the amount of tourism receipts experiences skyrocketed until 2008, after a flat trend from 1995 to 2001. The Global Financial Crises caused a relatively insignificant fall, after which the receipts per capita starts to rise again. However, there was a new fall in tourism in 2014. According to the World Bank, as of 2015, Albania and Nepal are the leaders in the consumption of electricity from renewable energy sources among other BRI countries included in the sample. The lowest share of renewables in electricity use is in Jordan and Belarus.

Table 2. Correlation matrix

	CO_2	RE	TOU	GDP	FDI	TR
CO_2	1					
RE	-0.521	1				
TOU	0.425	-0.155	1			
GDP	0.710	-0.358	0.788	1		
FDI	0.207	-0.155	0.272	0.281	1	
TR	0.408	-0.243	0.557	0.693	0.432	1

Methodology

Unit-Root Procedures

The approach chosen for the current analysis is based on the existence of cointegration among variables. Pedroni (1999) states that cointegration exists under the assumption that, in case of conventional time-series, some set of variables are first order integrated and can be described as stationary. To reach the stationarity of selected variables, following Isaeva et al. (2021), the study

employed Im, Pesaran and Shin (2003) unit root test (IPS). In contrast with
Levin–Lin–Chu (2002), the IPS test applies separate unit-root test for each of
the N cross-section units. The test has general form of:

$$\Delta y_{it} = \varphi_i y_{i(t-1)} + \sigma_i x_{it} + \epsilon_{it} \qquad (2)$$

Where y_{it} and x_{it} denote the individual and combination of regressors; φ is
specific for each panel i, while in LLC test this term is constant; i=1,...N and
t=1,...T denotes a country and time period respectively. The assumption of
the test is that the number of time periods, T, is fixed. Further it assumes that
the error term is normally and independently distributed for all panels i and
year t as well as allowing error term variance to be heterogeneous across
panels. To check the robustness of the IPS unit-root estimates, the study
follows Maddala and Wu (1999) and applies the Fisher-type Augmented
Dickey-Fuller (ADF) procedure and Phillips-Perron unit-root test.

Cointegration Procedures

As far as the stationarity of the variables is reached it allows to perform a
cointegration analysis. Following Zoundi (2017), we employ Pedroni (1999),
Kao (1999) and Westerlund (2005) cointegration procedures. The Pedroni
(1999) cointegration approach uses the specific parameters to account for
heterogeneity and allows variation across individual panels. The test has the
general form of:

$$y = \alpha_i + \beta_{1i} x_{1i,t} + \beta_{2i} x_{2i,t} + \cdots + \beta_{Mi} x_{Mi,t} + e_{i,t} \qquad (3)$$

Where i=1,...N; t=1,...T; and m=1...M denote a country, time period and a
particular regressor, respectively.

The Pedroni cointegration procedure estimates contain seven statistics,
including within-panel and group tests. According to Nguyen and Kakinaka
(2019), the within-panel test "proposes a common autoregressive coefficient
across cross-sections, while the between-dimension test assumes an individual
autoregressive coefficient for each cross-section." In the case that one or more
regressors are non-stationary, the panel is considered heterogeneous. Further,
we perform Kao (1999) and Westerlund (2005) to check the robustness of the
obtained cointegration estimates. While the Kao test applies similar techniques

as Pedroni tests, for this test it is necessary for the coefficients of regressors to be homogeneous as well as it is necessary to have cross-section specific intercepts. The Westerlund (2005) cointegration procedure uses the model where the AR parameter is panel-specific. The alternative hypothesis of the test is that the series in some of the panels are cointegrated.

In the case of the existence of cointegrated long-run relationships among variables, it is of interest to identify the direction of the integration. To test it, the study follows Khan et al. (2019) and applies Fully Modified ordinary least squares procedure developed by Pedroni (2001). The significant advantage of this approach is that it accounts for endogeneity bias and the existence of serial correlation. For panels with heterogenous cointegration, it is considered the most relevant procedure (Hamit-Haggar, 2012).

Finally, we are interested in the investigation of possible causal association among variables. Following Isaeva et al. (2021), we perform a Dumitrescu and Hurlin (2012) Granger non-causality test. The test is applicable for balanced and heterogeneous panels, and accounts for the presence of cross-sectional dependence. Moreover, the procedure can be employed in both cases when T > N and T < N. The test has the following general form:

$$z_{i,t} = \alpha_i + \sum_{k=1}^{K} \lambda_{ik} z_{i,t-k} + \sum_{k=1}^{K} \beta_{ik} x_{i,t-k} + \varepsilon_{i,t} \tag{4}$$

Where λ_{ik} is the autoregressive parameter and β_{ik} is the coefficient of regression varying within the groups for a particular country i in period t.

The testing of the null hypothesis of no causality against the alternative one is based on the use of a z-bar and z-bar tilde statistics. The last one is more valid in case of relatively small sample size and period. The problem of lag selection is better to be solved based on the information criterion (AIC/BIC/HQIC).

Results and Discussion

The results of the panel unit-root procedures are provided in Table 3. Most of the variables are non-stationary according to the IPS procedure. The detrending of the variables allows us to reach stationarity of all variables with

Table 3. Panel unit root test results

Variable	Form	Method	Statistic	P-value	Conclusion
ln CO$_2$	Level	IPS	3.345	1.000	Non stationary
		Fisher-ADF	96.575	0.164	Non stationary
		Fisher-PP	70.026	0.863	Non stationary
	1st difference	IPS	-13.385	0.000	Stationary
		Fisher-ADF	371.305	0.000	Stationary
		Fisher-PP	714.555	0.000	Stationary
ln Renewable energy	Level	IPS	-0.301	0.382	Non stationary
		Fisher-ADF	126.536	0.002	Stationary
		Fisher-PP	127.323	0.002	Stationary
	1st difference	IPS	-14.253	0.000	Stationary
		Fisher-ADF	579.797	0.000	Stationary
		Fisher-PP	856.845	0.000	Stationary
ln Tourism	Level	IPS	1.383	0.917	Non stationary
		Fisher-ADF	51.562	0.998	Non stationary
		Fisher-PP	77.234	0.686	Non stationary
	1st difference	IPS	-13.404	0.000	Stationary
		Fisher-ADF	374.653	0.000	Stationary
		Fisher-PP	688.702	0.000	Stationary
ln GDP per capita	Level	IPS	9.227	1.000	Non stationary
		Fisher-ADF	39.331	1.000	Non stationary
		Fisher-PP	31.025	1.000	Non stationary
	1st difference	IPS	-8.394	0.000	Stationary
		Fisher-ADF	241.558	0.000	Stationary
		Fisher-PP	322.521	0.000	Stationary

Variable	Form	Method	Statistic	P-value	Conclusion
ln Squared GDP per capita	Level	IPS	10.193	1.000	Non stationary
		Fisher-ADF	36.961	1.000	Non stationary
		Fisher-PP	27.682	1.000	Non stationary
	1st difference	IPS	-8.294	0.000	Stationary
		Fisher-ADF	238.621	0.000	Stationary
		Fisher-PP	317.365	0.000	Stationary
ln FDI	Level	IPS	-6.680	0.000	Stationary
		Fisher-ADF	192.454	0.000	Stationary
		Fisher-PP	230.579	0.000	Stationary
	1st difference	IPS	-15.691	0.000	Stationary
		Fisher-ADF	561.207	0.000	Stationary
		Fisher-PP	1125.517	0.000	Stationary
ln Trade	Level	IPS	0.211	0.584	Non stationary
		Fisher-ADF	102.490	0.083	Stationary
		Fisher-PP	79.394	0.622	Non stationary
	1st difference	IPS	-12.749	0.000	Stationary
		Fisher-ADF	411.028	0.000	Stationary
		Fisher-PP	595.342	0.000	Stationary

statistically significant coefficients. Based on the results of IPS and Fisher-type procedures, variables can be considered as mixed order integrated (Bekun et al., 2018). To obtain economically and statistically meaningful coefficients of the independent variables, the indicators should be either stationary or cointegrated at their levels. Thus, the study further employs panel cointegration procedures to test the existence of long-run association among variables.

The results of the Pedroni, Kao and Westerlund cointegration procedures are shown in Table 4. The cointegration is proven by both panel and group statistics at 1% significance level, with exception to Panel rho-statistic where significance level is 10%. Further, the robustness check performed by applying the Kao ADF approach also supports the existence of cointegrated relationships. However, the Westerlund Variance Ratio does not support this conclusion.

Table 4. Pedroni, Kao and Westerlund panel cointegration results

	Statistics
V-stat	-4.389***
Panel rho-stat	2.234*
Panel PP-stat	-12.24***
Panel ADF-stat	5.991***
Group rho stat	4.38 ***
Group PP stat	-14.14 ***
Group ADF stat	7.609***
Kao (ADF)	-12.9602***
Westerlund Variance Ratio	1.2075

Note: ***, ** and * indicate significance at 1%, 5% and 10% levels, respectively.

Table 5. FMOLS estimation results (dependent variable: CO_2)

	FMOLS	OLS	FE
lnTOU	0.03***	0.0861737	-0.001
lnRE	-0.17***	-0.137***	-0.043***
lnGDP	9.33	6.814***	4.701***
lnGDP^2	-0.44	-0.308***	-0.233***
lnFDI	-0.02**	1.155***	0.389 ***
lnTR	0.02***	-0.157***	0.006

Note: ***, ** and * indicate significance at 1%, 5% and 10% levels, respectively and figures in parentheses are t-statistic.

Since the existence of cointegration among variables is proven, it is possible to determine the direction of this cointegration based on the FMOLS approach. The results presented in Table 5 show that the amount of tourism receipts are positively associated with the level of carbon dioxide emission at 1% significance level. A 1% increase in tourism receipts is associated with a 0.03% rise in CO_2 emission levels. These results are in line with findings proposed by Haseeb and Azam (2020). On the other hand, the share of renewable energy in total electricity output demonstrates the negative effect on CO_2 emission with elasticity of carbon emission of -0.17%. These results are quite logical and are proven by several previous studies, including Jebli et al. (2016), Hu et al. (2018) and Jin and Kim (2018). Notably, the analysis does not provide statistically significant evidence on the validity of the Environmental Kuznets Curve in the countries during the observed period. These results conflict with Hu et al. (2018), Dogan and Inglesi-Lotz (2020), and Kirikkaleli and Kalmaz (2020). The validity of the EKC is proven by the OLS and fixed-effects procedure results, while providing contradictory results for main explanatory variables. These findings agree with studies documented by Olale et al. (2018) and Armeanu et al. (2018).

Now we turn to the final part of our analysis where we are interested in the determination of causal association among variables. The results of the Dumitrescu and Hurlin (2012) panel Granger non-causality procedure are shown in Table 6. The findings document unidirectional causality from carbon emission level to the share of renewables in electricity output. This finding suggests that an increased level of environmental degradation forces governments to encourage the expansion of renewables in energy generation. Similar conclusions are supported by the studies conducted by Luni and Majeed (2020), Jaforullah and King (2015), and Musah et al. (2020) in case of lower- and lower-middle-income countries. However, such findings contradict the results proposed by Khattak et al. (2020), Dong et al. (2018) and Inglesi-Lotz and Dogan (2018).

Further, the results demonstrate the existence of bidirectional causal relationships between tourism and carbon emission level. The results support one of the previous findings on the carbon-tourism association proposed by Paramati et al. (2017). The feedback association between these variables can be explained in the following way: the touristic attractiveness of a particular country stimulates the sectors of transportation, entertainment, and hotel businesses, which are energy intensive. The increased energy consumption drives CO_2 emission, especially in those countries where traditional energy sources are dominant. At the same time, an increased level of carbon emission and a corresponding reduction in air quality can negatively affect the reputation of the country as the center of tourism. Further, the findings document the unidirectional strand moving from national income to development of the sector of tourism. Similar results are provided by Dogan and Aslan (2017) in the case of EU and candidate countries, as well as by Zhang and Liu (2019) in the case of the Northeast and Southeast Asian regions. However, the obtained results are in conflict with findings provided by Roudi et al. (2019) and Blien et al. (2017), who document the bidirectional causal linkage between tourism and GDP, and Gao et al. (2019) and Akadiri and Akadiri (2019), whose findings report the unidirectional strand from tourism to GDP.

Table 6. Dumitrescu and Hurlin (2012) Panel Granger non-causality test results

Dependent variable	Independent variables					
	ln CO_2	*lnRE*	*lnTOU*	*lnGDP*	*lnFDI*	*lnTR*
ln CO_2		1.540 (0.124)	1.898* (0.058)	1.533 (0.125)	-1.152 (0.249)	-1.064 (0.287)
lnRE	1.831* (0.067)		0.434 (0.664)	1.060 (0.2892)	1.300 (0.194)	0.895 (0.371)
lnTOU	3.086*** (0.002)	-1.025 (0.305)		2.914*** (0.004)	-0.3973 (0.691)	1.013 (0.311)
lnGDP	0.566 (0.571)	-0.131 (0.896)	0.505** (0.613)		-0.369 (0.712)	0.063 (0.950)
lnFDI	0.771 (0.441)	-1.123 (0.262)	0.194 (0.846)	1.488 (0.137)		-0.6328 (0.527)
lnTR	1.413 (0.158)	1.349 (0.177)	0.598 (0.550)	0.983 (0.326)	-0.879 (0.379)	

Note: ***, ** and * indicate significance at 1%, 5% and 10% levels, respectively.

Conclusion and Policy Implications

This chapter provides the evidence on the long-run cointegrated relationship between carbon emission, renewable energy, and tourism development in the case of BRI countries from 1995 to 2015. The findings of Pedroni (1999) and Kao (1999) prove the existence of long-run cointegrated relationships between chosen variables at 1% significance level. Further, the FMOLS procedure documents the statistically significant positive long-term association between CO_2 emission and tourism receipts. The obtained results are consistent with findings provided by Khan et al. (2020) and Haseeb and Azam (2020).

The findings of this study have various policy implications. Given that increased energy consumption is strongly linked to climate change and carbon emissions, tourism-oriented countries must implement suitable measures to limit tourism-induced energy use. One of the possible solutions would be for policymakers to offer an incentive for key stakeholders in the tourism sector to use cleaner energy, carbon-neutral transportation, and hybrid energies in order to achieve the targeted level of carbon emission reductions.

The fact that the tourism industry is mainly dominated by transportation activities makes this sector one of the most important factors affecting the natural environment. Rico et al., (2019) stated in his research that almost 95% of tourism-related CO_2 emissions belong to transport services, mainly from aviation. Based on the achieved results, it is highly recommended to design sustainable tourism policies in the case of the transportation sector. Considering previous empirical findings in this research field, tourism-oriented countries should utilize alternative fuel or hybrid engines in both air and other transport services. According to Raza et al. (2017), low-cost air travel can be viewed as an alternative solution because it creates hypermobile travel models. This policy will help to decrease the damaging effect of tourism activities and also help enhance tourism's contribution to countries in terms of economic growth.

As the number of visitors to a country grows, the range of infrastructural services, such as lodging, hotels, restaurants, airports, ports, highways, and railroads will increase respectively. All these buildings include heating or air conditioning facilities which has a considerable cost in terms of CO_2 emissions (Lenzen et al., 2018). It is highly recommended for the accommodation industry to transform the energy sources into solar or wind energy technologies. The government might offer tax breaks or low-cost (e.g., interest-free) financing for the purchase and installation of renewable energy sources as incentive.

Some scholars have explored the importance of investment in tourism industry for the sake of sustainable development (Paramati et al., 2018). The tourism sector can be development within the scope of investment-oriented tourism, which will motivate investors to construct roads, organize recycling programs in touristic facilities, and support renewable energy and other projects in order to achieve green infrastructure. Developing green tourism is not only beneficial to the environment but also to a nation's economy as well. In order to reduce the impact of urbanization in rural areas, it is highly suggested by experts to save forests, as they are main contributors of clean environment.

Finally, international cooperation should be strengthened among the countries, which will increase the ability to mitigate the acceleration of climate change unilaterally. Achieving the SDGs by 2030 is the most important course of action for all members of the agreement to have a clean and sustainable world. Moreover, environmentally sustainable tourism should be maintained not only by society, but also by individuals, increasing their awareness and knowledge about how their choices impact the environment.

This study has following limitation which is the agenda for future research. First, it is important to assess the role of tourism in promoting wellbeing and economic progress as sub-national level for countries located in the Belt and Road Region. Moreover, it would be useful to explore whether environmental awareness is higher in tourism-oriented regions of Belt and Road Initiative countries. This would imply that tourism has indirect effect on sustainable development via changes in cultural values.

References

Adams, S., & Nsiah, C. (2019). Reducing carbon dioxide emissions; Does renewable energy matter? *Science of the Total Environment*, *693*, 133288. https://doi.org/10.1016/j.scitotenv.2019.07.094.

Akadiri, S. S., & Akadiri, A. C. (2019). Examining the causal relationship between tourism, exchange rate, and economic growth in tourism island states: evidence from second-generation panel. *International Journal of Hospitality & Tourism Administration*, 1-16.

Akram, R., Chen, F., Khalid, F., Ye, Z., & Majeed, M. T. (2020). Heterogeneous effects of energy efficiency and renewable energy on carbon emissions: Evidence from developing countries. *Journal of Cleaner Production*, *247*, 119122. https://doi.org/10.1016/j.jclepro.2019.119122.

Amelung, B., Nicholls, S., & Viner, D. (2007). Implications of global climate change for tourism flows and seasonality. *Journal of Travel research*, *45*(3), 285-296.

Anderson, T. R., Hawkins, E., & Jones, P. D. (2016). CO_2, the greenhouse effect and global warming: from the pioneering work of Arrhenius and Callendar to today's Earth System Models. *Endeavour*, *40*(3), 178-187.

Armeanu, D., Vintilă, G., Andrei, J. V., Gherghina, Ş. C., Drăgoi, M. C., & Teodor, C. (2018). Exploring the link between environmental pollution and economic growth in EU-28 countries: Is there an environmental Kuznets curve?. *PloS one*, *13*(5), e0195708.

Aydoğan, B., & Vardar, G. (2019). Evaluating the role of renewable energy, economic growth and agriculture on CO 2 emission in E7 countries. *International Journal of Sustainable Energy*, *0*(0), 1–14. https://doi.org/10.1080/14786451.2019.1686380.

Balli, E., Sigeze, C., Manga, M., Birdir, S., & Birdir, K. (2019). The relationship between tourism, CO 2 emissions and economic growth: a case of Mediterranean countries. *Asia Pacific Journal of Tourism Research, 24*(3), 219–232. https://doi.org/10.1080/10941665.2018.1557717.

Baloch, M. A., Mahmood, N., & Zhang, J. W. (2019). Effect of natural resources, renewable energy and economic development on CO_2 emissions in BRICS countries. *Science of the Total Environment, 678,* 632-638.

Balsalobre-Lorente, D., & Leitão, N. C. (2020). The role of tourism, trade, renewable energy use and carbon dioxide emissions on economic growth: evidence of tourism-led growth hypothesis in EU-28. *Environmental Science and Pollution Research, 27*(36), 45883–45896. https://doi.org/10.1007/s11356-020-10375-1.

Basarir, C., & Cakir, Y. N. (2015). Causal Interactions Between Co2 Emissions, Financial Development, Energy and Tourism. *Asian Economic and Financial Review, 5*(11), 1227–1238. https://doi.org/10.18488/journal.aefr/2015.5.11/102.11.1227.1238.

Bekun, F. V., Alola, A. A., & Sarkodie, S. A. (2019). Toward a sustainable environment: Nexus between CO_2 emissions, resource rent, renewable and nonrenewable energy in 16-EU countries. *Science of the Total Environment, 657,* 1023–1029. https://doi.org/10.1016/j.scitotenv.2018.12.104.

Ben Jebli, M., Ben Youssef, S., & Apergis, N. (2019). The dynamic linkage between renewable energy, tourism, CO_2 emissions, economic growth, foreign direct investment, and trade. *Latin American Economic Review, 28*(1). https://doi.org/10.1186/s40503-019-0063-7.

Bilgili, F., Koçak, E., Bulut, Ü., & Kuloğlu, A. (2017). The impact of urbanization on energy intensity: Panel data evidence considering cross-sectional dependence and heterogeneity. *Energy, 133,* 242–256. https://doi.org/10.1016/j.energy.2017.05.121.

Bilen, M., Yilanci, V., & Eryüzlü, H. (2017). Tourism development and economic growth: a panel Granger causality analysis in the frequency domain. *Current Issues in Tourism, 20*(1), 27-32.

Countries, M. E. (2021). *Renewable Energy and CO2 Emissions: Empirical Evidence from Major Energy-Consuming Countries.* 1–10.

D'Alessandro, F. (2016). Green Building for a Green Tourism. A New Model of Eco-friendly Agritourism. *Agriculture and Agricultural Science Procedia, 8,* 201–210. https://doi.org/10.1016/j.aaspro.2016.02.094.

Danish, Baloch, M. A., Mahmood, N., & Zhang, J. W. (2019). Effect of natural resources, renewable energy and economic development on CO_2 emissions in BRICS countries. *Science of the Total Environment, 678,* 632–638. https://doi.org/10.1016/J.SCITOTENV.2019.05.028.

Dumitrescu, E. I., & Hurlin, C. (2012). Testing for Granger non-causality in heterogeneous panels. *Economic modelling, 29*(4), 1450-1460.

Dogan, E., & Aslan, A. (2017). Exploring the relationship among CO_2 emissions, real GDP, energy consumption and tourism in the EU and candidate countries: Evidence from panel models robust to heterogeneity and cross-sectional dependence. *Renewable and Sustainable Energy Reviews, 77*(February), 239–245. https://doi.org/10.1016/j.rser.2017.03.111.

Dogan, E., & Seker, F. (2016). Determinants of CO_2 emissions in the European Union: the role of renewable and non-renewable energy. *Renewable Energy, 94*, 429-439.

Dogan, E., Seker, F., & Bulbul, S. (2017). Investigating the impacts of energy consumption, real GDP, tourism and trade on CO_2 emissions by accounting for cross-sectional dependence: A panel study of OECD countries. *Current Issues in Tourism, 20*(16), 1701–1719. https://doi.org/10.1080/13683500.2015.1119103.

Dogan, E., & Inglesi-Lotz, R. (2020). The impact of economic structure to the environmental Kuznets curve (EKC) hypothesis: evidence from European countries. *Environmental Science and Pollution Research, 27*(11), 12717-12724.

Dong, K., Hochman, G., Zhang, Y., Sun, R., Li, H., & Liao, H. (2018). CO_2 emissions, economic and population growth, and renewable energy: Empirical evidence across regions. *Energy Economics, 75*, 180-192.

Eyuboglu, K., & Uzar, U. (2020). The impact of tourism on CO_2 emission in Turkey. *Current Issues in Tourism, 23*(13), 1631–1645. https://doi.org/10.1080/13683500.2019.1636006.

Gao, J., Xu, W., & Zhang, L. (2019). Tourism, economic growth, and tourism-induced EKC hypothesis: evidence from the Mediterranean region. *Empirical Economics*, 1-23.

Gössling, S., Garrod, B., Aall, C., Hille, J., & Peeters, P. (2011). Food management in tourism: Reducing tourism's carbon "foodprint." *Tourism Management, 32*(3), 534–543. https://doi.org/10.1016/j.tourman.2010.04.006.

Gössling, S., Scott, D., & Hall, C. M. (2015). Inter-market variability in CO_2 emission-intensities in tourism: Implications for destination marketing and carbon management. *Tourism Management, 46*, 203–212. https://doi.org/10.1016/j.tourman.2014.06.021.

Hamit-Haggar, M. (2012). Greenhouse gas emissions, energy consumption and economic growth: A panel cointegration analysis from Canadian industrial sector perspective. *Energy Economics, 34*(1), 358-364.

Haseeb, M., & Azam, M. (2020). Dynamic nexus among tourism, corruption, democracy and environmental degradation: a panel data investigation. *Environment, Development and Sustainability*, 1-19.

Hu, H., Xie, N., Fang, D., & Zhang, X. (2018). The role of renewable energy consumption and commercial services trade in carbon dioxide reduction: Evidence from 25 developing countries. *Applied energy, 211*, 1229-1244.

Huang Y., Kuldasheva Z., Salahodjaev R. Renewable Energy and CO_2 Emissions: Empirical Evidence from Major Energy-Consuming Countries. *Energies*. 2021; 14(22):7504. https://doi.org/10.3390/en14227504.

Ikram, M., Zhang, Q., Sroufe, R., & Shah, S. Z. A. (2020). Towards a sustainable environment: The nexus between ISO 14001, renewable energy consumption, access to electricity, agriculture and CO_2 emissions in SAARC countries. *Sustainable Production and Consumption, 22*, 218–230. https://doi.org/10.1016/j.spc.2020.03.011.

Im, K. S., Pesaran, M. H., & Shin, Y. (2003). Testing for unit roots in heterogeneous panels. *Journal of econometrics, 115*(1), 53-74.

Inglesi-Lotz, R., & Dogan, E. (2018). The role of renewable versus non-renewable energy to the level of CO_2 emissions a panel analysis of sub-Saharan Africa's Big 10 electricity generators. *Renewable Energy,* 123, 36-43.

Isaeva, A., Salahodjaev, R., Khachaturov, A., & Tosheva, S. (2021). The Impact of Tourism and Financial Development on Energy Consumption and Carbon Dioxide Emission: Evidence from Post-communist Countries. *Journal of the Knowledge Economy,* 1-14.

Jaforullah, M., & King, A. (2015). Does the use of renewable energy sources mitigate CO_2 emissions? A reassessment of the US evidence. *Energy Economics,* 49, 711-717.

Jebli, M. B., Youssef, S. B., & Ozturk, I. (2016). Testing environmental Kuznets curve hypothesis: The role of renewable and non-renewable energy consumption and trade in OECD countries. *Ecological Indicators,* 60, 824-831.

Jin, T., & Kim, J. (2018). What is better for mitigating carbon emissions–Renewable energy or nuclear energy? A panel data analysis. *Renewable and Sustainable Energy Reviews,* 91, 464-471.

Kao, C. (1999). Spurious regression and residual-based tests for cointegration in panel data. *Journal of econometrics,* 90(1), 1-44.

Katircioglu, S. T. (2014b). International tourism, energy consumption, and environmental pollution: The case of Turkey. *Renewable and Sustainable Energy Reviews,* 36, 180-187.

Katircioglu, S. T., Feridun, M., & Kilinc, C. (2014). Estimating tourism-induced energy consumption and CO_2 emissions: The case of Cyprus. *Renewable and Sustainable Energy Reviews,* 29, 634–640. https://doi.org/10.1016/j.rser.2013.09.004.

Khan, M. W. A., Panigrahi, S. K., Almuniri, K. S. N., Soomro, M. I., Mirjat, N. H., & Alqaydi, E. S. (2019). Investigating the dynamic impact of CO_2 emissions and economic growth on renewable energy production: Evidence from FMOLS and DOLS tests. *Processes,* 7(8), 496.

Khan, A., Chenggang, Y., Hussain, J., Bano, S., & Nawaz, A. (2020). Natural resources, tourism development, and energy-growth- CO_2 emission nexus: A simultaneity modeling analysis of BRI countries. *Resources Policy,* 68, 101751.

Khanal, A., Rahman, M. M., Khanam, R., & Velayutham, E. (2021). Is tourism and energy consumption linked? Evidence from australia. *Sustainability (Switzerland),* 13(19). https://doi.org/10.3390/su131910800.

Khattak, S. I., Ahmad, M., Khan, Z. U., & Khan, A. (2020). Exploring the impact of innovation, renewable energy consumption, and income on CO_2 emissions: new evidence from the BRICS economies. *Environmental Science and Pollution Research,* 1-16.

Kirikkaleli, D., & Kalmaz, D. B. (2020). Testing the moderating role of urbanization on the environmental Kuznets curve: empirical evidence from an emerging market. *Environmental Science and Pollution Research,* 27(30), 38169-38180.

Koçak, E., Ulucak, R., & Ulucak, Z. Ş. (2020). The impact of tourism developments on CO_2 emissions: An advanced panel data estimation. *Tourism Management Perspectives,* 33(October 2019). https://doi.org/10.1016/j.tmp.2019.100611

Leitão, N. C., & Lorente, D. B. (2020). The linkage between economic growth, renewable energy, tourism, CO_2 emissions, and international trade: The evidence for the European Union. *Energies,* 13(18), 4838.

Lenzen, M., Sun, Y. Y., Faturay, F., Ting, Y. P., Geschke, A., & Malik, A. (2018). The carbon footprint of global tourism. *Nature Climate Change*, 8(6), 522–528. https://doi.org/10.1038/s41558-018-0141-x.

Levin, A., Lin, C. F., & Chu, C. S. J. (2002). Unit root tests in panel data: asymptotic and finite-sample properties. *Journal of econometrics,* 108(1), 1-24.

Luni, T., & Majeed, M. T. (2020). Improving environmental quality through renewable energy: evidence from South Asian economies. *International Journal of Energy and Water Resources,* 4, 335-345.

Menyah, K., & Wolde-Rufael, Y. (2010). CO_2 emissions, nuclear energy, renewable energy and economic growth in the US. *Energy policy,* 38(6), 2911-2915.

Musah, M., Kong, Y., Mensah, I. A., Antwi, S. K., & Donkor, M. (2020). The link between carbon emissions, renewable energy consumption, and economic growth: a heterogeneous panel evidence from West Africa. *Environmental Science and Pollution Research,* 27, 28867-28889.

Nguyen, K. H., & Kakinaka, M. (2019). Renewable energy consumption, carbon emissions, and development stages: Some evidence from panel cointegration analysis. *Renewable Energy,* 132, 1049-1057.

Olale, E., Ochuodho, T. O., Lantz, V., & El Armali, J. (2018). The environmental Kuznets curve model for greenhouse gas emissions in Canada. *Journal of cleaner production,* 184, 859-868.

Owusu, P. A., & Asumadu-Sarkodie, S. (2016). A review of renewable energy sources, sustainability issues and climate change mitigation. *Cogent Engineering,* 3(1), 1167990.

Paramati, S. R., Alam, M. S., & Chen, C. F. (2017). The Effects of Tourism on Economic Growth and CO_2 Emissions: A Comparison between Developed and Developing Economies. *Journal of Travel Research*, 56(6), 712–724. https://doi.org/10.1177/0047287516667848.

Paramati, S. R., Alam, M. S., & Lau, C. K. M. (2018). The effect of tourism investment on tourism development and CO_2 emissions: empirical evidence from the EU nations. *Journal of Sustainable Tourism,* 26(9), 1587–1607. https://doi.org/10.1080/09669582.2018.1489398.

Pedroni, P. (1999). Critical values for cointegration tests in heterogeneous panels with multiple regressors. Oxford Bulletin of Economics and statistics, 61(S1), 653-670.

Raza, S. A., Sharif, A., Wong, W. K., & Karim, M. Z. A. (2017). Tourism development and environmental degradation in the United States: evidence from wavelet-based analysis. *Current Issues in Tourism,* 20(16), 1768–1790. https://doi.org/10.1080/13683500.2016.1192587.

Rico, A., Martínez-Blanco, J., Montlleó, M., Rodríguez, G., Tavares, N., Arias, A., & Oliver-Solà, J. (2019). Carbon footprint of tourism in Barcelona. *Tourism Management,* 70(March 2018), 491–504. https://doi.org/10.1016/j.tourman.2018.09.012.

Roudi, S., Arasli, H., & Akadiri, S. S. (2019). New insights into an old issue–examining the influence of tourism on economic growth: evidence from selected small island developing states. *Current Issues in Tourism,* 22(11), 1280-1300.

Sadorsky, P. (2009). Renewable energy consumption, CO_2 emissions and oil prices in the G7 countries. *Energy Economics*, 31(3), 456-462.

Saidi, K., & Omri, A. (2020). Reducing CO_2 emissions in OECD countries: Do renewable and nuclear energy matter? *Progress in Nuclear Energy*, *126*(February), 103425. https://doi.org/10.1016/j.pnucene.2020.103425.

Shafiei, S., & Salim, R. A. (2014). Non-renewable and renewable energy consumption and CO_2 emissions in OECD countries: a comparative analysis. *Energy Policy*, 66, 547-556.

Sghaier, A., Guizani, A., Ben Jabeur, S., & Nurunnabi, M. (2019). Tourism development, energy consumption and environmental quality in Tunisia, Egypt and Morocco: a trivariate analysis. *Geo Journal*, *84*(3), 593–609. https://doi.org/10.1007/s10708-018-9878-z.

Shahnazi, R., & Dehghan Shabani, Z. (2021). The effects of renewable energy, spatial spillover of CO_2 emissions and economic freedom on CO_2 emissions in the EU. *Renewable Energy*, *169*, 293–307. https://doi.org/10.1016/j.renene.2021.01.016.

Shakouri, B., Khoshnevis Yazdi, S., & Ghorchebigi, E. (2017). Does tourism development promote CO_2 emissions? *Anatolia*, *28*(3), 444–452. https://doi.org/10.1080/13032917.2017.1335648.

Solarin, S. A. (2014). Tourist arrivals and macroeconomic determinants of CO_2 emissions in Malaysia. *Anatolia*, *25*(2), 228–241. https://doi.org/10.1080/13032917. 2013.868364.

Wolde-rufael, Y., & Weldemeskel, E. M. (2020). Environmental policy stringency, renewable energy consumption and CO_2 emissions : Panel cointegration analysis for BRIICTS countries Environmental policy stringency, renewable energy consumption and CO 2 emissions : *International Journal of Green Energy*, *00*(00), 1–15. https://doi.org/10.1080/15435075.2020.1779073.

Zhang, S., & Liu, X. (2019). The roles of international tourism and renewable energy in environment: new evidence from Asian countries. *Renewable energy*, 139, 385-394.

Zhang, J., & Zhang, Y. (2021). Tourism, economic growth, energy consumption, and CO_2 emissions in China. *Tourism Economics*, *27*(5), 1060–1080. https://doi.org/10. 1177/1354816620918458.

Zoundi, Z. (2017). CO_2 emissions, renewable energy and the Environmental Kuznets Curve, a panel cointegration approach. *Renewable and Sustainable Energy Reviews*, 72, 1067-1075.

Chapter 7

Socio-Economic Correlates of Depression in Russia

Askarova Feruza[*]

Tashkent State University of Economics, Tashkent, Uzbekistan

Abstract

Current study analyzes the socio-economic correlates of depression in Russia between 2011 and 2018. The data is driven by eight waves of the Russian Longitudinal Monitoring Survey (RLMS). Independent variables are divided into three categories: individual characteristics, health and health-related characteristics, and economic variables. Coefficients are derived from OLS, Logit, and Probit regressions. Our findings suggest that marriage, having children, a higher education, employment, a good state of health, and better financial situation decrease the risk of experiencing a nervous disorder or depression. The effect of age is nonlinear and concave, so exposure to depression increases at earlier life stages and then decreases once an individual's age reaches 41.

Keywords: mental health, depression, Russia

---

[*] Corresponding Author's Email: askarova.f1@gmail.com.

In: Economic Growth and Wellbeing
Editor: Raufhon Salahodjaev
ISBN: 978-1-68507-990-1
© 2022 Nova Science Publishers, Inc.

Introduction

Depression is the most widespread mental disorder in the world. Between 1990 and 2017, it has been seizing the world progressively and in 2017, more than 260 million people of all ages suffer from depression.[1] Depression greatly reduces an individual's overall state of health, decreases daily functioning, and can lead to disability and premature death. Apart from productivity loss, physical health worsening, and the risk of suicide, significant financial resources are required for mental disorder treatment including medicine, therapeutic and medical services, and hospital stays among many other possible expenses (Hu et al., 2007).

Historically, mental health was not treated as a big concern of public policies in Russia. Although individuals with mental health problems were supported by legislation in 1992, a lack of resources was the impediment to fulfilling this obligation (Jenkins et al., 2007). In the 1990s, the federal Urgent Measures for Improving Psychiatric Care program received only 0.2% of Russia's GDP and thus was unable to properly provide services. At the same time, Russia represents an interesting research topic in this context due to its complex development path. The Soviet Union collapse, and the post-collapse crisis was followed by significant socio-economic and political reforms and rapid growth. Moreover, between 1990 and 2015, several setbacks occurred, including a Global Financial Crisis and oil price shocks. Finally, in 2014, imposed international sanctions cost Russia $40 billion over the course of a year, and the freefalling oil industry another $100 billion (Wade & Cairney, 1997; Rutland, 2014), which impacted the well-being of the country significantly. Such substantial political and economic transformations shape unique patterns of a nation's well-being and mental health.

As depression negatively affects people's physical health and emotional well-being, it also brings negative economic consequences, thereby highlighting the need for the development of mental health services. Negative economic outcomes of depression often worsen as a result of social stigma, restricted access to mental health services, lack of health insurance; yet the monetary impact may be minimized and even prevented by rapid diagnosis and treatment. In this sense, significant opportunities for policy implementation exist; yet, reducing the negative economic outcomes as well as preventing or treating depressive disorder requires policymakers and authorities to be aware of its correlates. Since depression is a complex and

---

[1] WHO, 2020. https://www.who.int/news-room/fact-sheets/detail/depression

multi-level phenomenon, the best course of action is to tackle its magnitude and extent by considering its main triggers and personal circumstances (Falicov, 2003).

Academia has been studying depression extensively, considering its various causes from different viewpoints, including biological, psychological, cultural, and socio-economic. Dunn et al. (2015) discus the role of an individual's genetic risks for depression and their interaction with a positive or negative environment. Gene structure does not predict depression directly, but it determines an individual's ability to cope with adverse life events. Although studies confirm the existence of genetic risks for depression, the interplay of those genetics with stressful life events can either exacerbate or buffer the negative effects of stress and can either raise or restrain depressive symptoms. A positive environment, on the contrary, assumes social and psychological support instead of stress. Following similar arguments, Assareh et al. (2015), introduces a model of "stress-induced biological changes resulting in depression following bereavement." An extreme early life stressor, such as bereavement or malnutrition, causes epigenetic changes and gene expression that progress in result of later life stressful events. As a result of gene expression and stress-related impact on the neuroendocrine and immune systems, the level of related proteins modifies, affecting the brain regions involved in in the development of depressive behavior (Assareh et al., 2015).

The biological nature of depression has also been studied in the context of gender. Altemus (2006) explains the greater instances of depression in females by biological means: "Processes which may contribute to increased rates of affective disorders in women are greater fluxes in reproductive hormones across the life span, and increased sensitivity to catecholamine augmentation of emotional memory consolidation." Goodwin & Gotlib (2004) employ the Big Five factor model to investigate the relationship between mental disorders and gender through personality traits and neuroticism in 3,000 adults in USA. Depressive symptoms are proxied by the short form of Composite International Diagnostic Interview. Results of logistic regression demonstrate that females are more prone to depression, anxiety, and panic attacks compared to males. However, the impact of life events and socio-economic circumstances should not be disregarded, since depression in females is also exacerbated by female poverty, exposure to sexual harassment, burden of care, and stress due to limited socio-economic activity (Nolen-Hoeksema et al., 1999). Although some hormonal changes at puberty can indeed cause limbic system hyperactivity in females, which consequently exacerbates negative emotional stimuli and increase depression risks, such effects are aggravated by socio-economic and cultural factors (Parker & Brotchie, 2010).

Some studies consider the emotional and psychological factors for depression. According to O. E. Lee & Ryu (2018), the emotions of pride and regret contribute slightly to depression. However, the intensity of the effect of such self-conscious emotions on depression is largely dependent on culture. For instance, the stronger the family values in a given society, the stronger the feelings of regrets over family conflicts. Yeonjung Lee & Bierman, (2019) investigate the relationship between loneliness, discrimination, and depressive symptoms in 7 thousand seniors. Results from random and fixed effects regression show that daily-life discrimination is associated with greater feelings of loneliness, which in turn enhances depression.

As it was already mentioned, physical environment is of particular importance when understanding the contributing factors of depression. Low socioeconomic status has been associated with greater susceptibility to psychiatric and mental diseases, disability, and restricted access to healthcare. Studying psychiatric disorders on a sample of US data, Kessler et al. (1994), noted that the prevalence of them decline as socioeconomic status increases. S. Weich & Lewis (1998), contributed to the research by studying the effect of low material living standards on mental disorder prevalence, using data on 9 thousand adults in England, Wales, and Scotland. Their findings imply that higher instances of mental disorders are associated with low material living standards, low income, and lack of savings.

In a meta-analysis perspective, Lorant et al. (2003), analyzed 51 studies, employing a random effects model and meta-regression. Socio-economic factors such as education, income, occupation, social class, and assets are considered. The results demonstrate that individuals whose social status is relatively lower are more prone to depression. Later, Lorant et al. (2007) observed that changes in socio-economic factors alter levels of depression. The authors employed data from seven-waves of a Belgian Household Panel Survey and various socio-economic factors, including annual income, savings, assets ownership, education, employment, and social relationships. A modified global depression scale was used to measure the level of depression. Fixed effects regression results demonstrate that financial difficulties and poverty exacerbates depressive symptoms and even leads to major depression. The cessation of cohabitation with a partner enhances depression risk as well.

Similar to Weich & Lewis (1998) and Lorant et al. (2007), Gillen et al. (2017), highlighted the significance of financial means in depression risk, exploring the relationship in a sample of 5000 adults using Ordinary Least

Squares hierarchical regression. Financial constraints are represented as debt, financial support from family members, and public assistance program participation. The model also controls for the extent to which an individual has control over their financial resources. Depression is assessed using a modified 8-item Center for Epidemiologic Studies Depression Scale. As an aggregated measure, financial constraints were positively associated with depression in middle-age and late life, and this relationship was partially accounted for by the pathway of perceived control over one's financial circumstances. Empirical findings reveal a significant positive association between financial difficulty at an individual level and depression. The effect is significant with financial control incorporated.

Depression determinants have been investigated in different populations: students, elderly, migrants, and homosexual males. Steptoe et al. (2007), explores depression factors in 17,348 students from 23 countries using the Beck Depression Inventory. Depression is described with macroeconomic, socio-economic, and cultural factors, including GDP, income inequality, age, gender, family wealth, parents' education, sense of control, access to education, and individualism/collectivism. The results demonstrate the importance of socio-economic background and a low sense of control in determining the risk of depression. Moreover, depression is higher in individuals from countries with larger income inequality and more collectivistic cultures.

Y. Lee et al., (2018) found the depression-moderating effect of social inclusion in a panel data sample of adult Korean population. Major determinants of depression are pre-existing depressive symptoms, health, and family support. Hsiao & Chen (2018) explored the effects of individual, family and external factors on depression in aged population in senior care-centers of Taiwan. Individual factors include gender, education, age, income, marital status, state of health, physical mobility, chronic diseases, etc. Family factors representing the extent of family cohesion were measured as the number of visits by family members, while external factors accounted for social interaction (participation in leisure activities, interaction with care-center residents, interaction with neighbors and other). The results demonstrate that major factors associated with depressive symptoms are chronic diseases, individuals' health and physical mobility. Similarly, S.-W. Lee et al. (2020), highlighted the importance of quality family relationships in preventing depressive disorders in the elderly Koreans between 2006-2013. Recently, Lim et al. (2020) observed that among senior adults in Korea, females, individuals with chronic diseases, and those who have no home are exposed to major and chronic depression.

Fenta et al. (2004) investigated risk factors for depressive disorder in a sample of 340 immigrants and refugees from Ethiopia in Toronto. Depressive disorder is measured by the Composite International Diagnostic Interview – a standardized interview developed by the World Health –Organization. Pre- and post-migration stress was considered as well by asking respondents about their experience in a refugee camp, duration of the stay, reason for immigration, and any traumatic events which might have happened to them before migrating. Sociodemographic characteristics, such as age, marital status, age at emigration and current migration status, language proficiency, education, religion, and employment status were also noted. Their findings revealed that lifetime depression prevalence in Ethiopian immigrants and refugees is greater than depression prevalence in Ontario and Southern Ethiopia. Moreover, for younger individuals, pre and post-migration stress and refugee camp experiences increase the risk of depression. Kim & Chen (2011) extended the research by examining social depression determinants in 148 elderly Korean immigrants in Toronto. The study accounts for acculturation issues and hypothesizes that adjusting to a new environment is more difficult for elderly populations, which consequently increases the risk of depressive symptoms. Socio-economic determinants, on the other hand, also play an important role. In particular, low levels of social integration, living alone, poor health, and financial difficulties increase the risk of depression. Pereira et al., (2020) studied the depression factors and trends in sexual minority older males from Spain and Portugal. Similar to previous studies, health and social relationships are significant predictors of depression.

Methods

Data and Variables

This particular study investigates the socio-economic correlates of depression by using data coming from the Russian Longitudinal Monitoring Survey (RLMS), introduced by the Higher School of Economics (HSE). It represents a series of national representative surveys conducted on an annual basis. The unified dataset includes more than 350 thousand observations between 1994 and 2018, not including 1997 and 1999 when the survey was not conducted.

The RLMS collects individual and household-level data on income and expenses structure, financial well-being, work and migration behavior, health, nutrition, education, leisure, and psychological well-being for the same group people over a long period of time. As a whole, it provides an opportunity to draw up a multidimensional picture of the Russian population. Our sample includes over 100 thousand observations.

Depression

Depression-related research has been regularly conducted since 2011, so we are restricting our analyses between 2011-2018. RLMS measures depression by item *M131*, which asks if the respondent has had a serious nervous disorder or depression within the past 12 months. The following responses are "Yes" or "No." We generated a binary variable, *depressed,* which equals to one for those who answered positively to the item *M131.*

More than 150 thousand individuals responded to depression-related questions. From 2011 to 2018, the share of individuals who experienced nervous disorder or depression had decreased from 9.5 percent in 2011 to 8.9 percent in 2018 (Figure 1). In our sample, approximately 11 percent of individuals experienced depression during the last year (Table 1).

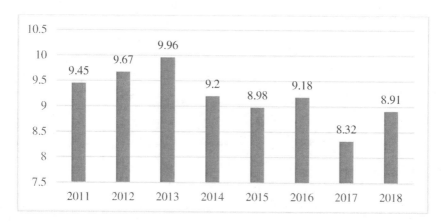

Figure 1. Share of depressed respondents between 2011-2018.

Individual-Level Covariates

We have divided independent variables into three categories. The first category considers individual characteristics such as gender, age, settlement type, education, marital and parental status. In our sample, 58 percent of subjects are females, and the average age is 50 years. We also account for non-linearity of age profile, which is discussed in depression literature by Mirowsky and Ross (1992) and Blazer et al., (1991), by including squared values of age into a regression equation. The majority (68 percent) of our sample live in urban rather than rural areas, and only 25 percent have a university degree. 61 percent are either registered as married or living with a partner, and 74 percent have children of their own or adopted children.

The second group of variables accounts for health and health-related behavior. According to Frerichs et al. (1982), physical illness is significantly related to depressive disorder. RLMS allows us to evaluate an individual's state of health by asking the respondent to estimate it using a 5-point scale, where 1 is "very bad" and 5 is "very good." According to Table 1, respondents were more or less satisfied with their health as the mean health score is 3.2. *Sport* is a dummy variable which is equal to one, measuring how much an individual is involved in light, medium, or intensive physical exercise on a regular basis. 28 percent of our sample participate in regular sports. As Paperwalla et al., (2004) states, depression increases the chances of smoking while smoking, at the same time, increases the likelihood of the development of depression. Boden et al., (2010) observed the causal relationship between nicotine-dependence and depression. The variable *smoker* equals to 1 if a person currently smokes. Nearly 29 percent of the participants are smokers (Table 1).

Table 1. Summary statistics

Variable	Description	Mean	Std. Dev.
Depressed	Dummy variable for experiencing nervous disorder or depression during the last 12 months; 0 otherwise	0.11	0.31
Female	Dummy variable for being female	0.58	0.49
Age	Age expressed in years	49.84	18.56
Urban	Dummy variable for living in urban areas	0.68	0.46
Education	Dummy variable for having university degree	0.25	0.43
Married	Dummy variable for being married	0.61	0.49
Children	Dummy variable for having a child/child	0.74	0.44
Health	1 is "very bad" and 5 is "very good."	3.25	0.73
Sport	Dummy variable for being engaged in physical activities	0.28	0.45
Smoker	Dummy variable for being a smoker	0.29	0.45
Employed	Dummy variable for being employed	0.53	0.50
Income	Total amount of money personally received in the last 30-day including wages, retirement pensions, premiums, profits, material aid, incidental earnings, and other receipts.	18879.47	30579.82
Financial situation	Imagine a nine-step ladder where on the bottom, the first step, stand the poorest people, and on the highest step, the ninth, stand the richest. On which step of the nine steps are you personally standing today?	3.98	1.46

The last category introduces economic variables which are employment status, personal income, and financial status. The former two are included in the Assari's (2017) analyses of depression determinants. Zimmerman and Katon (2005) also observed that income is significantly associated with depression. We have generated a binary variable, *employed,* to account for the effect of having a job. 53 percent of respondents in our sample are employed and the average income is 18.8 thousand rubles. It should be noted that income represents the total amount of money personally received in the last 30-days including wages, retirement pensions, premiums, profits, material aid, incidental earnings, and other receipts. Financial situation is closely related to income, but it allows interpersonal comparison. The variable is generated from item *J61,* which asks respondents to place themselves on a nine-step ladder, with the richest people at the top and the poorest at the bottom. On average, individuals place themselves on the fourth step (Table 1).

Econometric Model

To investigate depression correlates, the following equation is estimated:

$$D_{i,j} = \alpha_0 + \sum_{k=1}^{6} \alpha_k I_{i,j} + \sum_{l=1}^{3} \alpha_l H_{i,j} + \sum_{m=1}^{3} \alpha_m E_{i,j} + \varepsilon_{i,j} \quad (1)$$

where D is a binary variable for being depressed for individual i in period j, k is a set of variables accounting for individual characteristics (I), l – for health and health-related behavior (H), and m – for economic variables (E). Similar to Assari (2017), binary dependent variables encourage the model to be estimated with Logistic and Probit regression. However, we are reporting the results of the Ordinary Least Squares regression as well, since the coefficients are easier to interpret. After reporting the estimates of Eq.1, we split the sample by income and gender categories. Our analyses are based on 28 subjects of the Russian Federation over 7 years.[2] Therefore, we are including year and region fixed effects in all regressions.

---

[2] Altai Krai, Amur oblast, Chelyabinsk oblast, Chuvash Republic, Kabardino-Balkar Republic, Kaluga oblast, Republic of Komi, Krasnodar Krai, Kurgan oblast, Leningrad oblast, Moscow city, Moscow oblast, Novosibirsk oblast, Orenburg oblast, Penza oblast, Perm Krai, Primosky Krai, Rostov oblast, Saratov oblast, Smolensk oblast, Stavropol Krai, Tambov oblast, Republic of Tatarstan, Tomsk oblast, Tula oblast, Tver oblast, Udmurt Republic, Volgograd oblast.

Empirical Analyses

All analyses conducted in Stata 15.0. Table 2 represents the main results. We have included categories of independent variables in a stepwise manner. The last two columns provide Logit and Probit regression results. Table 3 provides the results of OLS regressions by gender and income categories.

As we expected, the relationship between age and depression is non-linear and concave at p<0.01. The coefficient is robust in different gender and income groups (Table 3). The threshold age is 41 years.

Table 2. Socio-economic correlates of depression

	OLS			Logit	Probit
Female	0.042***	0.041***	0.038***	0.503***	0.265***
	(0.002)	(0.002)	(0.002)	(0.024)	(0.013)
Age	0.005***	0.003***	0.004***	0.040***	0.021***
	(0.000)	(0.000)	(0.000)	(0.004)	(0.002)
Age sq.	-0.000***	-0.000***	-0.000***	-0.000***	-0.000***
	(0.000)	(0.000)	(0.000)	(0.000)	(0.000)
Urban	-0.040***	-0.044***	-0.044***	-0.416***	-0.211***
	(0.004)	(0.004)	(0.004)	(0.038)	(0.021)
University degree	-0.029***	-0.017***	-0.012***	-0.143***	-0.074***
	(0.002)	(0.002)	(0.002)	(0.026)	(0.013)
Married	-0.033***	-0.028***	-0.026***	-0.258***	-0.141***
	(0.002)	(0.002)	(0.002)	(0.024)	(0.013)
Children	-0.012***	-0.008***	-0.006**	-0.071**	-0.035**
	(0.003)	(0.003)	(0.003)	(0.032)	(0.017)
Health		-0.088***	-0.086***	-0.905***	-0.478***
		(0.002)	(0.002)	(0.017)	(0.009)
Sport participation		0.006***	0.006***	0.072***	0.041***
		(0.002)	(0.002)	(0.024)	(0.013)
Smoker		0.026***	0.026***	0.329***	0.175***
		(0.002)	(0.002)	(0.026)	(0.013)
Employed			-0.038***	-0.365***	-0.197***
			(0.003)	(0.026)	(0.014)
Income, natural log			0.002***	0.020***	0.011***
			(0.000)	(0.004)	(0.002)
Financial status			-0.004***	-0.039***	-0.020***
			(0.001)	(0.008)	(0.004)
_cons	-0.061***	0.316***	0.307***	-0.410***	-0.292***
	(0.009)	(0.011)	(0.012)	(0.137)	(0.072)
N	127797	123980	117681	117681	117681
adj. R^2	0.051	0.081	0.081		

Robust standard errors in parentheses.
All regressions include year and region dummy variables.
* p<0.1, ** p<0.05, *** p<0.01.

General correlates which are positively associated with depression are gender, sports, smoking, and income. According to our data, females are more likely to experience nervous disorder or depression at $p<0.01$, supporting the findings of Weissman and Klerman (1985), who observe that depressive symptoms are twofold higher in females compared to their counterparts.

Although some physical activities have been considered as lessening the effects of depression (Antonelli, 1982), and sport participation may be effective in the treatment of nervous disorders (Fox, 1999; Warburton, 2006), our study supports the opposite. Those who are engaged in sports are 0.6 percent more likely to get depressed. However, the coefficient of sport participation is insignificant in males and relatively poor individuals (Table 3).

In line with Paperwalla et al., (2004), smoking increases the probability of depression. In our sample, smokers are 2.9 percent more likely to experience depression. The results stay robust in different gender and income categories (Table 3). Surprisingly, higher personal incomes increase depression risk at $p<0.05$; however, in relatively rich respondents, the coefficient is insignificant (Table 3).

Settlement type, high education, marriage, parenthood, health, employment, and financial situation decrease depression risk. Those who live in urban areas are 4 percent less likely to get depressed and individuals with a university degree are less prone to depression as well at $p<0.01$ (Table 2, 3).

Marriage also decreases the chance of depression. Married individuals are less prone to nervous disorders or depression, which is in line with Inaba et al., (2005) and Kessler and Essex (1982), who explained that single individuals are less resilient to psychological harm and stressful life events. The effect of marriage is strong and negative in females and males, as well as in richer and poorer respondents.

McLanahan and Adams (1987) explained that parenthood may be positively related to depression, yet our results support the opposite. The coefficient of *children* is negative and significant at $p<0.01$. Interestingly, the coefficient loses its power in Table 3, in the sense that having children is not related to depression in males and relatively rich individuals in our sample. Further, health is negatively and significantly related to depression, meaning that better physical health decreases the likelihood of getting depressed.

Zimmermann and Katon (2005) state that unemployment causes depression. In our study, employed individuals are 3.8 percent less prone to depression. Neither gender nor income makes a difference. Finally, the way in which individuals estimate their own financial situation compared to the richest and the poorest significantly related to the prevalence of nervous disorders and depression. Our results suggest that one step closer to the richest tier decreases the likelihood of depression by 0.4 percent at p<0.01, other things being equal, yet the coefficient is insignificant in relatively rich respondents.

Table 3. Socio-economic correlates of depression: sub-sampling

	Gender categories		Income categories	
	Females	**Males**	**Below mean income**	**Above mean income**
Female			0.046***	0.035***
			(0.000)	(0.000)
Age	0.003***	0.004***	0.006***	0.003***
	(0.000)	(0.001)	(0.001)	(0.000)
Age sq.	-0.000***	-0.000***	-0.000***	-0.000***
	(0.000)	(0.000)	(0.000)	(0.000)
Urban	-0.048***	-0.040***	-0.039***	-0.044***
	(0.006)	(0.005)	(0.009)	(0.005)
University degree	-0.020***	0.001	-0.002	-0.013***
	(0.003)	(0.003)	(0.007)	(0.002)
Married	-0.023***	-0.036***	-0.031***	-0.037***
	(0.003)	(0.004)	(0.008)	(0.002)
Children	-0.009**	-0.001	0.017**	-0.002
	(0.004)	(0.004)	(0.009)	(0.003)
Health	-0.094***	-0.073***	-0.083***	-0.087***
	(0.002)	(0.002)	(0.004)	(0.002)
Sport participation	0.006**	0.003	0.003	0.006***
	(0.003)	(0.003)	(0.005)	(0.002)
Smoker	0.039***	0.020***	0.039***	0.005**
	(0.004)	(0.003)	(0.006)	(0.002)
Employed	-0.030***	-0.050***	-0.025***	-0.041***
	(0.003)	(0.004)	(0.008)	(0.003)
Income, natural log	0.002***	0.003***	0.002***	0.000
	(0.001)	(0.001)	(0.001)	(0.002)
Financial status	-0.004***	-0.003***	-0.000	-0.004***
	(0.001)	(0.001)	(0.001)	(0.001)
_cons	0.383***	0.250***	0.221***	0.413***
	(0.016)	(0.017)	(0.029)	(0.023)
N	68,468	49,213	20,304	97,377
adj. R^2	0.078	0.079	0.082	0.079

Robust standard errors in parentheses.
All regressions include year and region dummy variables.
Regressions estimated with Ordinary Least Squares.
* p<0.1, ** p<0.05, *** p<0.01.

Discussion and Conclusion

The ever-increasing prevalence of depression and its associated economic costs prompts more research interest in to its contributing factors; yet the evidence is limited in the case of Russia. Our study analyzes socio-economic correlates of depression using data on Russian individuals between 2011 and 2018. In our study, depression is modeled by individual characteristics, health and health-related behavior, and economic variables. Empirical results are reported with Ordinary Least Squares (OLS), Logit, and Probit regressions.

Consistent with previous research (Girgus & Yang, 2015), our findings suggest that females are more exposed to nervous disorders and depression. This may be explained by both biological differences between males and females and hormonal changes in females, as well as socio-economic and cultural factors such as greater care-burden, physical violence, and poverty. Moreover, although gender discrimination is not obvious in Russia, women are fired first and often receive lower pay for the same education and experience versus men (Averina et al., 2005).

The effect of age is nonlinear and concave, so the risk of depression increases at earlier life stages and then decreases once an individual's age reaches 41. Mirowsky & Ross (1992) observed a non-linear convex relationship between age and depression. A higher risk of depression later in life is explained by bereavement, job loss, decreasing economic well-being, and a decline in health. As for Russia, Salahodjaev & Ibragimova (2020) observed that self-reported life satisfaction declines until approximately 43 years and then increases, suggesting a convex relationship. As nervous disorders and depression are negatively related to life satisfaction, we can state that an individual's mental well-being in Russia tends to lower at earlier life stages, and rise at middle age of around 41 to 43 years.

Individuals living in urban areas are less prone to depression in Russia. Although modern research suggests that living in urban areas is negatively related to mental health due to negative physical environments and industrial pollution (Wade & Cairney, 1997), lower depression risk in our sample may be explained by relatively higher economic and infrastructure developments in urban areas in Russia. Another factor which decreases depression risk in our sample is higher education. Education and any learning activities may improve an individual's physical and mental health, as it increases the ability of an individual to process information and allows individuals to make more considered decisions (Chevalier & Feinstein, 2006). Marriage and parenthood also decrease depression exposure, as it increases an individual's resilience to adverse life events (Helbig et al., 2006; Inaba et al., 2005; Kessler and Essex, 1982). Moreover, cultural values play a vital role in the relationship between marriage, parenthood, and depression. In this context, Russia is for the most part a conservative, family-oriented nation (McKenzie et al., 2013).

Physical health as an important contributor to mental health and depression has been abundantly researched in persons with physical health problems (Bardone et al., 1998; Moussavi et al., 2007; Pilling et al., 2009; Shen et al., 2011). On the one hand, depressed individuals are more prone to physical illnesses (Frerichs et al., 1982); while, on the other, individuals who suffer from chronic disease are more vulnerable to depression (Moussavi et al., 2007). In our study, state of physical health reduces the risk of depressive disorder, which supports the findings of Averina et al., (2005). Smoking and sport participation, on the contrary, increases depression risk. Although depression itself may initiate smoking, smoking also triggers the development of depressive symptoms (Paperwalla et al., 2004). There are biological mechanisms behind a smoking addiction, as nicotine impacts the brain region responsible for mood elevation, attention, memory, and information processing, yet smokers are more likely to experience depression at some point in life (Quattrocki et al., 2000). On the topic of Russia, unhealthy habits such as smoking and alcohol consumption worsens depression (Averina et al., 2005). As for sports, our results suggest that individuals engaged in sports are more likely to experiences nervous or depressive disorder. Sport participation generally decreases depressive symptoms (Antonelli, 1982), yet some studies point out that unique stressors are experienced by athletes which may threaten their mental health (Donohue et al., 2018). One potential reason for such a negative relationship in our study is the measurement of sport in RLMS, which does not allow for a proper account of the intensity of engagement in sports.

Finally, economic variables, such as employment status, personal income, and financial status are significantly related to depression in Russia. During major economic and political transformations, individual economic stability is of great concern. Employment is an important factor of mental health and general well-being in Russia (Frijters et al., 2006) and our findings support previous studies. Although a higher income generally improves an individual's well-being, our findings suggest the opposite. Interestingly, income is not related to depression in relatively rich individuals. Existing research provides support for a positive relationship between income and depression due to discriminative behavior towards some populations (Assari & Caldwell, 2018). As for Russia, a negative relationship between depression and income may be explained by extensive working hours and unique stressors which are common in high-income occupations. Finally, the relative financial situations of individuals are considered. (Van Praag, 2011) explained that, besides individual characteristics, individual well-being is largely dependent on the so-called "referencing process" or, in other words, the process of comparison with others. Our research demonstrates that the closer people estimate their financial position to the richest people in their society, the lower the risk for depression.

Our findings include some interesting policy suggestions. Firstly, a greater focus of concern should be dedicated to the mental health of the Russian population and its correlates, and mental services require proper reflection and reassessment in the national healthcare agenda. Secondly, depressive symptoms may be tackled in part by helping to mitigate common socio-economic factors, such as ensuring equal rights and opportunities for higher education, promoting higher education for the youth, encouraging healthy lifestyles and smoking cessation. It is also important to assure the financial security of the population by reducing income inequality and strengthening social security policies. Employment services and job creation measures may also decrease the risk of individuals developing nervous disorders or depression.

Although our study sheds light on the socio-economic factors contributing to depression in Russia, it has several shortcomings. Firstly, our analyses provide significant and robust results, yet they are not causal. Further studies are recommended to employ more sophisticated econometric techniques in order to analyze a causal relationship. Second, the RLMS accounts for nervous disorder and depressive symptoms by a simple yes/no question, which does not allow for incorporating the severity of depression into analyses. Finally, social interaction is an important factor in moderating or preventing depression disorder and thus should be included in further investigation.

References

Altemus, M. (2006). Sex differences in depression and anxiety disorders: Potential biological determinants. *Hormones and Behavior, 50*(4), 534–538. https://doi.org/10.1016/j.yhbeh.2006.06.031.

Antonelli, F. (1982). Sport and depression therapy. *International Journal of Sport Psychology, 13*(3), 187–193.

Antonelli, F. (1982). Sport and depression therapy. *International Journal of Sport Psychology.*

Assareh, A. A., Sharpley, C. F., McFarlane, J. R., & Sachdev, P. S. (2015). Biological determinants of depression following bereavement. *Neuroscience & Biobehavioral Reviews, 49,* 171–181. https://doi.org/10.1016/j.neubiorev.2014.12.013.

Assari, S. (2017). Social determinants of depression: the intersections of race, gender, and socioeconomic status. *Brain Sciences, 7*(12), 156.

Assari, S., & Caldwell, C. H. (2018). High Risk of Depression in High-Income African American Boys. *Journal of Racial and Ethnic Health Disparities, 5*(4), 808–819. https://doi.org/10.1007/s40615-017-0426-1.

Averina, M., Nilssen, O., Brenn, T., Brox, J., Arkhipovsky, V. L., & Kalinin, A. G. (2005). Social and lifestyle determinants of depression, anxiety, sleeping disorders and self-evaluated quality of life in Russia. *Social Psychiatry and Psychiatric Epidemiology, 40*(7), 511–518. https://doi.org/10.1007/s00127-005-0918-x.

Bardone, A. M., Moffitt, T. E., Caspi, A., Dickson, N., Stanton, W. R., & Silva, P. A. (1998). Adult Physical Health Outcomes of Adolescent Girls With Conduct Disorder, Depression, and Anxiety. *Journal of the American Academy of Child & Adolescent Psychiatry, 37*(6), 594–601. https://doi.org/10.1097/00004583-199806000-00009.

Blazer, D., Burchett, B., Service, C., & George, L. K. (1991). The association of age and depression among the elderly: an epidemiologic exploration. *Journal of gerontology, 46*(6), M210-M215.

Boden, J. M., Fergusson, D. M., & Horwood, L. J. (2010). Cigarette smoking and depression: tests of causal linkages using a longitudinal birth cohort. *The British Journal of Psychiatry, 196*(6), 440-446.

Chevalier, A., & Feinstein, L. (2006). Sheepskin or Prozac: The Causal Effect of Education on Mental Health (SSRN Scholarly Paper ID 923530). *Social Science Research Network.* https://papers.ssrn.com/abstract=923530.

Donohue, B., Gavrilova, Y., Galante, M., Gavrilova, E., Loughran, T., Scott, J., Chow, G., Plant, C. P., & Allen, D. N. (2018). Controlled Evaluation of an Optimization Approach to Mental Health and Sport Performance. *Journal of Clinical Sport Psychology, 12*(2), 234–267. https://doi.org/10.1123/jcsp.2017-0054.

Dunn, E. C., Brown, R. C., Dai, Y., Rosand, J., Nugent, N. R., Amstadter, A. B., & Smoller, J. W. (2015). Genetic determinants of depression: Recent findings and future directions. *Harvard Review of Psychiatry, 23*(1), 1–18. https://doi.org/10.1097/HRP.0000000000000054.

Falicov, C. J. (2003). Culture, society and gender in depression. *Journal of Family Therapy, 25*(4), 371–387. https://doi.org/10.1111/1467-6427.00256.

Fenta, H., Hyman, I., & Noh, S. (2004). Determinants of Depression Among Ethiopian Immigrants and Refugees in Toronto. *The Journal of Nervous and Mental Disease, 192*(5), 363–372. https://doi.org/10.1097/01.nmd.0000126729.08179.07.

Fox, K. R. (1999). The influence of physical activity on mental well-being. *Public health nutrition, 2*(3a), 411-418.

Frerichs, R. R., Aneshensel, C. S., Yokopenic, P. A., & Clark, V. A. (1982). Physical health and depression: An epidemiologic survey. *Preventive Medicine, 11*(6), 639–646. https://doi.org/10.1016/0091-7435(82)90026-3.

Frijters, P., Geishecker, I., Haisken-DeNew, J. P., & Shields, M. A. (2006). Can the Large Swings in Russian Life Satisfaction be Explained by Ups and Downs in Real

Incomes?*. *The Scandinavian Journal of Economics, 108*(3), 433–458. https://doi.org/10.1111/j.1467-9442.2006.00459.x.

Gillen, M., Zurlo, K. A., & Kim, H. (2017). Do Financial Constraints Affect Depressive Symptomatology Among Mid-Aged and Older Adults? *The International Journal of Aging and Human Development, 85*(4), 438–455. https://doi.org/10.1177/0091415017697724.

Girgus, J. S., & Yang, K. (2015). Gender and depression. *Current Opinion in Psychology, 4*, 53–60. https://doi.org/10.1016/j.copsyc.2015.01.019.

Goodwin, R. D., & Gotlib, I. H. (2004). Gender differences in depression: The role of personality factors. *Psychiatry Research, 126*(2), 135–142. https://doi.org/10.1016/j.psychres.2003.12.024.

Helbig, S., Lampert, T., Klose, M., & Jacobi, F. (2006). Is parenthood associated with mental health? *Social Psychiatry and Psychiatric Epidemiology, 41*(11), 889–896. https://doi.org/10.1007/s00127-006-0113-8.

Hsiao, Y. C., & Chen, C. Y. (2018). Exploring Individual, Family, and Extrafamilial Factors Associated With Depression Among Elderly Residents of Care Settings. *The International Journal of Aging and Human Development, 86*(3), 219–241. https://doi.org/10.1177/0091415017699938.

Hu, T., He, Y., Zhang, M., & Chen, N. (2007). Economic costs of depression in China. *Social Psychiatry and Psychiatric Epidemiology, 42*(2), 110–116. https://doi.org/10.1007/s00127-006-0151-2.

Inaba, A., Thoits, P. A., Ueno, K., Gove, W. R., Evenson, R. J., & Sloan, M. (2005). Depression in the United States and Japan: gender, marital status, and SES patterns. *Social science & medicine, 61*(11), 2280-2292.

Jenkins, R., Lancashire, S., McDaid, D., Samyshkin, Y., Green, S., Watkins, J., Potasheva, A., Nikiforov, A., Bobylova, Z., & Gafurov, V. (2007). Mental health reform in the Russian Federation: An integrated approach to achieve social inclusion and recovery. *Bulletin of the World Health Organization, 85*, 858–866.

Kessler, R. C., & Essex, M. (1982). Marital status and depression: The importance of coping resources. *Social forces, 61*(2), 484-507.

Kessler, R. C., McGonagle, K. A., Zhao, S., Nelson, C. B., Hughes, M., Eshleman, S., Wittchen, H.-U., & Kendler, K. S. (1994). Lifetime and 12-Month Prevalence of DSM-III-R Psychiatric Disorders in the United States: Results From the National Comorbidity Survey. *Archives of General Psychiatry, 51*(1), 8–19. https://doi.org/10.1001/archpsyc.1994.03950010008002.

Kim, W., & Chen, Y.-L. (2011). The Social Determinants of Depression in Elderly Korean Immigrants in Canada: Does Acculturation Matter? *The International Journal of Aging and Human Development, 73*(4), 283–298. https://doi.org/10.2190/AG.73.4.a.

Lee, O. E., & Ryu, S. (2018). Effects of Pride and Regret on Geriatric Depression: A Cross-Cultural Study With Mixed-Methods Approaches. *The International Journal of Aging and Human Development, 86*(2), 152–171. https://doi.org/10.1177/0091415017697726.

Lee, S. W., Choi, J. S., & Lee, M. (2020). Life Satisfaction and Depression in the Oldest Old: A Longitudinal Study. *The International Journal of Aging and Human Development, 91*(1), 37–59. https://doi.org/10.1177/0091415019843448.

Lee, Yeonjung, & Bierman, A. (2019). Loneliness as a Mediator of Perceived Discrimination and Depression: Examining Education Contingencies. *The International Journal of Aging and Human Development, 89*(2), 206–227. https://doi.org/10.1177/0091415018763402.

Lee, Youjung, Jang, K., & Lockhart, N. C. (2018). Impact of Social Integration and Living Arrangements on Korean Older Adults' Depression: A Moderation Model. *The International Journal of Aging and Human Development, 86*(3), 306–321. https://doi.org/10.1177/0091415017720887.

Lim, H. J., Cheng, Y., Kabir, R., & Thorpe, L. (2020). Trajectories of Depression and Their Predictors in a Population-Based Study of Korean Older Adults. *The International Journal of Aging and Human Development*, 0091415020944405. https://doi.org/10.1177/0091415020944405.

Lorant, V., Deliège, D., Eaton, W., Robert, A., Philippot, P., & Ansseau, M. (2003). Socioeconomic Inequalities in Depression: A Meta-Analysis. *American Journal of Epidemiology, 157*(2), 98–112. https://doi.org/10.1093/aje/kwf182.

Lorant, Vincent, Croux, C., Weich, S., Deliège, D., Mackenbach, J., & Ansseau, M. (2007). Depression and socio-economic risk factors: 7-year longitudinal population study. *The British Journal of Psychiatry, 190*(4), 293–298. https://doi.org/10.1192/bjp.bp.105.020040.

McKenzie, K., Murray, A., & Booth, T. (2013). Do urban environments increase the risk of anxiety, depression and psychosis? An epidemiological study. *Journal of Affective Disorders, 150*(3), 1019–1024. https://doi.org/10.1016/j.jad.2013.05.032.

McLanahan, S., & Adams, J. (1987). Parenthood and psychological well-being. *Annual review of sociology, 13*(1), 237-257.

Mirowsky, J., & Ross, C. E. (1992). Age and depression. *Journal of health and social behavior*, 187-205.

Moussavi, S., Chatterji, S., Verdes, E., Tandon, A., Patel, V., & Ustun, B. (2007). Depression, chronic diseases, and decrements in health: Results from the World Health Surveys. *The Lancet, 370*(9590), 851–858. https://doi.org/10.1016/S0140-6736(07)61415-9.

Nolen-Hoeksema, S., Larson, J., & Grayson, C. (1999). Explaining the gender difference in depressive symptoms. *Journal of Personality and Social Psychology, 77*(5), 1061–1072. https://doi.org/10.1037/0022-3514.77.5.1061.

Paperwalla, K. N., Levin, T. T., Weiner, J., & Saravay, S. M. (2004). Smoking and depression. *Medical Clinics, 88*(6), 1483–1494. https://doi.org/10.1016/j.mcna.2004.06.007.

Parker, G., & Brotchie, H. (2010). Gender differences in depression. *International Review of Psychiatry, 22*(5), 429–436. https://doi.org/10.3109/09540261.2010.492391.

Pereira, H., de Vries, B., Serrano, J. P., Afonso, R. M., Esgalhado, G., & Monteiro, S. (2020). Depression and Quality of Life in Older Gay and Bisexual Men in Spain and Portugal. *The International Journal of Aging and Human Development, 91*(2), 198–213. https://doi.org/10.1177/0091415019864600.

Pilling, S., Anderson, I., Goldberg, D., Meader, N., & Taylor, C. (2009). Depression in adults, including those with a chronic physical health problem: Summary of NICE guidance. *BMJ, 339*, b4108. https://doi.org/10.1136/bmj.b4108.

Quattrocki, E., Baird, A., & Yurgelun-Todd, D. (2000). Biological Aspects of the Link between Smoking and Depression. *Harvard Review of Psychiatry, 8*(3), 99–110. https://doi.org/10.1080/hrp_8.3.99.

Rutland, P. (2014). The impact of sanctions on Russia. *Russian Analytical Digest, 157*(1), 1-8.

Shen, B. J., Eisenberg, S. A., Maeda, U., Farrell, K. A., Schwarz, E. R., Penedo, F. J., Bauerlein, E. J., & Mallon, S. (2011). Depression and Anxiety Predict Decline in Physical Health Functioning in Patients with Heart Failure. *Annals of Behavioral Medicine, 41*(3), 373–382. https://doi.org/10.1007/s12160-010-9251-z.

Steptoe, A., ardle, J., Tsuda, A., & Tanaka, Y. (2007). Depressive symptoms, socio-economic background, sense of control, and cultural factors in University students from 23 Countries. *International Journal of Behavioral Medicine, 14*(2), 97–107. https://doi.org/10.1007/BF03004175.

Van Praag, B. (2011). Well-being inequality and reference groups: An agenda for new research. *The Journal of Economic Inequality, 9*(1), 111–127. https://doi.org/10.1007/s10888-010-9127-2.

Wade, T. J., & Cairney, J. (1997). Age and Depression in a Nationally Representative Sample of Canadians: A Preliminary Look at the National Population Health Survey. *Canadian Journal of Public Health, 88*(5), 297–302. https://doi.org/10.1007/BF03403892.

Warburton, D. E., Nicol, C. W., & Bredin, S. S. (2006). Health benefits of physical activity: the evidence. *Canadian Medical Associatetion Journal, 174*(6), 801-809.

Weich, S., & Lewis, G. (1998). Material standard of living, social class, and the prevalence of the common mental disorders in Great Britain. *Journal of Epidemiology & Community Health, 52*(1), 8–14. https://doi.org/10.1136/jech.52.1.8.

Weissman, M. M., & Klerman, G. L. (1985). Gender and depression. *Trends in Neurosciences, 8*, 416-420.

Zimmerman, F. J., & Katon, W. (2005). Socioeconomic status, depression disparities, and financial strain: what lies behind the income-depression relationship?. *Health economics, 14*(12), 1197-1215.

Chapter 8

Culture and Environmental Performance: The Case of Long-Term Orientation

Raufhon Salahodjaev[*]

Tashkent State University of Economics, Uzbekistan

Abstract

Environmental quality significantly varies across nations. The goal of this research is to assess how a given country's existing environmental performance is affected by one of the existing cultural dimensions, namely, long-term orientation. Our cross-country analysis shows that long-term orientation is significantly and positively related to the Environmental Performance index (EPI). For example, looking at the country with the lowest LTO in our sample versus highest is associated with a 13.4 point (nearly one standard deviation) increase in the EPI. The results are robust for a number of sensitivity tests.

Keywords: culture, long-term orientation, environmental performance

Introduction

Scholars and policymakers are in general agreement that environmental degradation has a negative impact on society. For example, deterioration of the environment has been linked to obesity (Liu et al., 2020), asthma (Bai et

---

[*] Corresponding Author's Email: Salahodjaev@gmail.com

In: Economic Growth and Wellbeing
Editor: Raufhon Salahodjaev
ISBN: 978-1-68507-990-1
© 2022 Nova Science Publishers, Inc.

al., 2022) and cancer mortality (Ruano-Ravina et al., 2021). Moreover, air pollution increases the risk of suicide (Ng et al., 2016) and reduces life satisfaction (Luechinger, 2010). While policymakers have committed to curb greenhouse gas emissions, reduce deforestation, and improve ecosystem vitality, the level of environmental performance across countries is highly unbalanced. For example, global CO_2 emissions increased from 20.6 million kilotons in 1990 to 34 million in 2018. India, China and the United States are the largest global emitters of CO_2 gas, while the small island countries of Tuvalu and Nauru contribute the least amount to the global rise in CO_2 emissions.[1]

Since the nineties, the amount of multidisciplinary research on the determinants of environmental degradation across nations has significantly increased. As a result, three major avenues of research have emerged. First, the role of economic factors in cross-country differences in environmental performance has been investigated. The main conclusion drawn from this research is that economic growth and energy consumption leads to a higher level of environmental degradation (Stern et al., 1996; Mirzaei & Bekri, 2017). A second avenue of research investigates the link between quality of institutions and environmental outcomes. In most of these papers, democracy index, corruption, rule of law, or economic freedom are used as proxies for the quality of institutions (Lv, 2017; Adesina & Mwamba, 2019). The third dimension of studies focuses on drivers of environmental degradation assesses the role of socio-cultural indicators. For example, patience, intelligence, trust, social capital, individualism and religiosity are used in modeling environmental performance across countries (Jo & Carrattini, 2021; Salahodjaev, 2018; Cai et al., 2020a; Cai et al., 2020b). The intentions of this study are to shed additional light on the long-run socio-cultural determinants of environmental degradation. Specifically, we are testing whether differences in long-term orientation may significantly explain cross-country differences in environmental performance.

As suggested by Bearden et al., (2006 p. 456), "long-term orientation (LTO) is a salient aspect of national culture values and as such influences [individual's] decision making processes." Moreover, long-term orientation is considered one of the 6 major Hofstede dimensions of culture. The Hofstede model suggests that "culture is the collective programming of the mind that distinguishes the members of one group or category of people from others" (Hofstede, 2011 p. 2308). Multi-disciplinary research has investigated

---

[1] https://data.worldbank.org/indicator/EN.ATM.CO2E.KT.

whether cultural differences vary in their impact on economic growth (Gorodnichenko and Roland (2017), life satisfaction (Mallard et al., 1997), and innovation (Efrat, 2014). However, this research largely focused on the individualistic/collectivistic dimension of culture, ignoring the long-term orientation. Moreover, to the best of our knowledge, no attempt has been taken to explore the effect of long-term orientation on environmental performance across different countries. The goal of our study is to fix this gap in the empirical literature.

Economic growth and market activities are considered paramount drivers of environmental degradation across different countries (Saboori et al., 2012). Thus, in markets where cultures give priority to short-term benefits, economic activities are more likely to increase environmental degradation. The longer the time orientation of society, the more likely it is that policymakers and companies will stress the importance of sustainable development with a lower ecological footprint. For example, Graafland (2020), using data for OECD countries, finds that long-term orientation enhances the effect of economic freedom on subjective wellbeing.

House et al., (2004 p. 12) defines LTO as "the degree to which individuals in organizations or societies engage in future-oriented behaviors such as planning, investing in the future, and delaying individual or collective gratification." In this context, LTO may strengthen environmental sustainability via "delay discounting," an aspect of decision-making in which individuals are willing to sacrifice smaller benefits available at the time in favor of long-term rewards (Matta et al., 2012). LTO has a positive impact on savings and innovations (Galor & Ozak, 2016), which in turn suggests that it will be related to more efficient environmental conservation. Moreover, studies show that LTO is positively related to non-monetary facets of human life such as the accumulation of human capital (House et al., 2004). Park and Jemaire (2011), using a GLS regression model for a sample of 27 countries, documented that LTO has a significant positive impact on demand for life insurance. Therefore, LTO societies are more likely to devote more resources to environmental health and design policies that are favorable for future generations. For example, Cai et al., (2020b) found that societies with higher levels of patience are more likely to ratify laws and regulations to mitigate climate change. Moreover, LTO has been positively linked to environmentally friendly consumer behavior (Gul, 2013) and investments in environmental practices (Durach and Wiengarten, 2017).

Empirical Strategy and Data

Empirical Model

We have estimated the following empirical model using cross-country data:

$$EP_i = \alpha + \beta LTO_i + \gamma' X_i + \varepsilon_i \tag{1}$$

where EP is the environmental performance (EP) in a country, and LTO is the long-term orientation measure in ith country, X is a set of control variables to reduce the omitted variable bias which includes GDP growth, democracy index, poverty rate, energy intensity and industry as % of GDP, and ε is a normally distributed error term. After discarding any missing observations, our sample contains 72 countries. We estimated Eq. (1) using ordinary a least squares (OLS) regression model with heteroskedasticity-adjusted robust standard errors.

Variables and Data Sources

Our dependent variable is the Environmental Performance Index (EPI) from Wendling et al., (2020). The composite EPI is estimated from 32 environmental indicators covering such areas as air quality, biodiversity and habitat, ecosystem services, pollution, climate change, and others. EPI calculates the level of environmental sustainability across countries and assesses how close countries are to established environmental policy targets. Methodologically, index scores range from 0 to 100, where higher values imply greater environmental sustainability. In our final sample, EPI scores range from 27.6 in India to 82.5 in Denmark.

To measure LTO, we relied on the Hofstede et al., (2010) dataset that offers data on long-term orientation scores for 84 societies (countries). The scores range from 0 (normative societies) to 100 (culture that takes a more pragmatic approach). Societies that score low exhibit a great respect for traditions, a relatively small propensity to save for the future, and a focus on achieving quick results.

In our regression modeling, we included a set of control variables that were suggested by extant research. First, in line with cross national studies on environmental degradation we included GDP growth as a proxy for the rate of economic growth (Cowan et al., 2014). The other control variables are democracy index, poverty, and energy intensity (Farzin & Bond, 2006; Masron & Subramaniam, 2019; Shahbaz et al., 2015). We have also included the share of industry in GDP as a proxy for manufacturing lobby. Table 1 provides summary statistics and variable sources and descriptions.

Table 1. Summary statistics, variable sources and descriptions

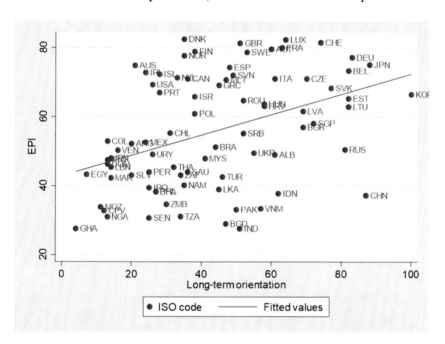

Empirical Results

Table 2 reports the baseline empirical estimates. Excluding control variables, LTO has a positive and significant (at the 1% level) association with the EPI (Column 1). For example, an increase in LTO by one standard deviation is associated with slightly less than a half standard deviation raise in the EPI. Moreover, LTO explains nearly 17% of cross-country variations in the EPI. Column 2 displays the estimates for the link between LTO and EPI after accounting for economic growth. While LTO is again positive and significant, GDP growth has a negative effect on the environmental performance. We further controlled for democracy (column 3) and poverty (column 4). In line with extant research, democratizations improve environmental quality, and poverty leads to greater environmental degradation (Masron & Subramaniam, 2019). The positive influence of LTO on the EPI is unaffected. We next controlled for energy intensity and the share of industry in GDP in columns 5 and 6. Of these two variables, only industrialization leads to environmental damage in our sample. The effect of LTO on environmental performance retains its positive sign and statistical significance at the 1% level. For example, moving from the country with the lowest LTO in our sample to the highest is associated with a 13.4 point (nearly one standard deviation) increase in the EPI.

Table 2. Main results

	I	II	III	IV	V	VI
LTO	0.2945	0.2110	0.2086	0.1508	0.1536	0.1425
	(4.65)***	(4.40)***	(4.26)***	(3.12)***	(3.02)***	(2.80)***
GDP growth		-4.7467	-3.8529	-3.0006	-2.8589	-2.3172
		(5.33)***	(4.12)***	(3.27)***	(3.11)***	(2.24)**
Democracy			0.8701	0.9468	1.0129	0.9615
			(3.43)***	(3.61)***	(3.84)***	(3.61)***
Poverty				-0.7180	-0.8093	-0.9980
				(3.90)***	(3.76)***	(5.05)***
Energy					0.4917	3.1731
					(0.15)	(0.88)
Industry						-0.3299
						(1.68)*
Constant	42.9632	63.7561	54.5374	55.8361	52.4634	48.5231
	(13.88)***	(14.53)***	(10.39)***	(11.09)***	(3.98)***	(3.64)***
R^2	0.17	0.44	0.52	0.62	0.63	0.64
N	79	79	77	74	72	72

Source; * $p < 0.1$; ** $p < 0.05$; *** $p < 0.01$.

Robustness Tests

Table 3 re-estimates Eq. (1) using alternative estimation techniques. One may argue that the OLS regression in Table 2 captures the effect of LTO on EPI, but that argument would overlook the effect of changing population size, which can also have effect on cultural values. Therefore, the weighted least squares (WLS) regression model is also an appropriate estimation method for our analysis. In column 1, we revisited our baseline results using WLS regression, where population size is used in assigning weights to each of the observations. The results show that LTO is positive and statistically significant, at the 5% level. In column 2, we used a robust regression (RREG) estimator which performs an initial screening based on Cook's distance > 1 to eliminate gross outliers, and then estimates the coefficients using Huber and bi-weight iterations. Finally, in column 3, we relied on a robust regression estimator, which fits the regression model using iteratively reweighted least squares (IRLS). Across all methods the coefficient for LTO is positive and statistically significant.

Table 3. Alternative estimators

	I	**II**	**III**
LTO	0.1517	0.1410	0.1532
	(2.41)**	(2.36)**	(3.24)***
GDP growth	-2.8082	-2.2734	-2.6199
	(3.12)***	(2.68)***	(2.12)**
Democracy	0.8140	1.0773	0.8591
	(2.56)**	(3.57)***	(3.00)***
Poverty	-1.0354	-0.9742	-1.0299
	(3.85)***	(3.94)***	(5.13)***
Energy	5.2474	2.9967	4.7192
	(1.44)	(0.90)	(1.07)
Industry	-0.3456	-0.3425	-0.3607
	(1.54)	(1.66)	(1.64)
Constant	41.8985	48.9540	43.7354
	(2.67)***	(3.41)***	(2.75)***
R^2	0.62	0.64	0.61
Estimator	WLS	RREG	IRWLS
N	72	72	72

Source: * $p < 0.1$; ** $p < 0.05$; *** $p < 0.01$.

In Table 4, we explored whether our main results may be affected by presence of influential or extreme data points in our sample. Extant research shows that outliers may have a significant effect on regression coefficients in cross-country studies (Shen et al., 2018). We excluded countries with the lowest and highest EPI scores in columns 1 and 2. In column 3, we removed countries with a population below 3 million people. Finally, we excluded outliers as suggested by the leverage-versus-squared-residual plot derived after OLS regression (column 4). The results are similar to our baseline findings.

At the same time, it is also important to consider the effect of other cultural dimensions and norms. For example, Jang et al., (2016) showed that uncertainty avoidance is negatively correlated with individualism. In Table 5, we included social trust and other dimensions of culture from the Hofstede model: Individualism, Masculinity, Power Distance (PD), Indulgence and Uncertainty Avoidance (UA). In line with extant studies, we found that trust and individualism are positively linked to environmental quality (Murtazashvili et al., 2019; Cai et al., 2020b). In contrast, PD and UA are negatively linked to EPI in our sample. Across all specifications, we still observed that LTO is positively related to EPI.

Table 4. Robustness test: extreme observations

	I	II	III	IV
LTO	0.1405	0.1254	0.1457	0.1321
	(2.86)***	(2.48)**	(2.99)***	(2.25)**
GDP growth	-1.8003	-2.2687	-3.2767	-1.9891
	(1.79)*	(2.21)**	(3.40)***	(1.69)*
Democracy	0.9973	0.9165	0.7848	1.0536
	(3.83)***	(3.57)***	(3.23)***	(3.81)***
Poverty	-0.9886	-1.0093	-1.1670	-1.0183
	(5.19)***	(5.35)***	(5.26)***	(4.72)***
Energy	3.3254	4.4120	2.7366	2.7102
	(0.96)	(1.22)	(0.79)	(0.63)
Industry	-0.3954	-0.2770	-0.1953	-0.3232
	(2.02)**	(1.47)	(1.01)	(1.47)
Constant	48.2507	41.3227	51.9244	49.8098
	(3.75)***	(3.10)***	(3.95)***	(3.02)***
R^2	0.63	0.64	0.68	0.65
Excluded countries	Bottom-3 by EPI	Top-3 by EPI	Population less than 3 million	Outliers (Ukraine and Mozambique)
N	69	69	70	63

Sourc: * p < 0.1; ** p < 0.05; *** p < 0.01.

Table 5. Robustness tests: other dimensions of culture

	I	II	III	IV	V	VI
LTO	0.0874	0.1221	0.1401	0.1521	0.2392	0.1465
	(2.07)**	(2.79)***	(2.81)***	(3.54)***	(4.61)***	(2.97)***
GDP growth	-2.3055	-1.9934	-2.3155	-2.0285	-2.0034	-3.0870
	(2.41)**	(2.45)**	(2.25)**	(2.73)***	(2.06)**	(2.91)***
Democracy	0.9915	0.6939	0.9535	0.7615	0.6548	0.9335
	(3.97)***	(3.52)***	(3.60)***	(4.06)***	(2.40)**	(3.59)***
Poverty	-0.8514	-0.5876	-1.0028	-0.7685	-1.0479	-1.0255
	(3.47)***	(3.35)***	(5.07)***	(4.16)***	(5.16)***	(5.09)***
Energy	-1.0318	-0.2689	3.2724	2.7590	3.0687	2.6121
	(0.31)	(0.09)	(0.92)	(0.85)	(0.93)	(0.72)

	I	II	III	IV	V	VI
Industry	-0.2327	0.0038	-0.3419	-0.0969	-0.3245	-0.2769
	(1.11)	(0.02)	(1.68)*	(0.50)	(1.71)*	(1.26)
Trust	35.8442					
	(5.90)***					
Individualism		0.3259				
		(5.69)***				
Masculinity			0.0266			
			(0.40)			
PD				-0.3157		
				(5.83)***		
Indulgence					0.2076	
					(2.93)***	
Uncertainty						-0.1483
						(2.43)**
Constant	57.9152	41.8411	47.2682	62.4935	36.5645	62.3806
	(4.97)***	(3.61)***	(3.44)***	(4.56)***	(2.56)**	(3.90)***
R^2	0.73	0.76	0.64	0.76	0.69	0.66
N	59	72	72	72	68	72

Source: * $p < 0.1$; ** $p < 0.05$; *** $p < 0.01$.

Conclusion

The goal of this study is to contribute to scholarly understanding of the relationship between culture and environmental degradation by focusing on the role of long-term orientation. We tested whether countries with higher levels of LTO are more likely to be associated with improved environmental performance. The results suggest that the LTO dimension of culture is positively, significantly, and robustly related to the EPI. Moreover, our study shows that LTO, irrespective of other cultural values and norms, is an important antecedent of environmental performance. Our results highlight that policymakers should consider the cultural variations across countries when developing strategies aimed at climate change mitigation.

Our results have a number of policy implications. Governments intending to institute policies aimed at increasing resilience against environmental degradation can succeed by strengthening long-term orientation of the citizens. With the existing uncertainty about negative impacts of climate change, long-termism is more likely to lead to environmental awareness and support for policies aimed at ecological conservation.

At the same time, prospective research should further assess the relationship between LTO and perceptions of climate change at individual levels in countries with high and low levels of LTO. There is also further need to explore the link between LTO and other environmental indicators for a larger set of countries. Finally, future studies should identify novel econometric methods that enable them to explore the causal effect of LTO on environmental degradation. Unfortunately, due to the data limitations, the use of more sophisticated empirical methods is not feasible in our study. Moreover, prospective studies should assess the effect of LTO on other macro-social indicators such as life satisfaction, inequality, trade and innovation.

References

Adesina, K. S., & Mwamba, J. W. M. (2019). Does economic freedom matter for CO2 emissions? Lessons from Africa. *The Journal of Developing Areas*, *53*(3).

Bai, S., Zhao, X., Liu, Y., Lin, S., Liu, Y., Wang, Z., ... & Wang, Z. (2022). The effect window for sulfur dioxide exposure in pregnancy on childhood asthma and wheezing: A case-control study. *Environmental Research*, *204*, 112286.

Bearden, W. O., Money, R. B., & Nevins, J. L. (2006). A measure of long-term orientation: Development and validation. *Journal of the Academy of Marketing Science*, *34*(3), 456-467.

Cai, M., Murtazashvili, I., Murtazashvili, J. B., & Salahodjaev, R. (2020a). Patience and climate change mitigation: Global evidence. *Environmental Research*, *186*, 109552.

Cai, M., Murtazashvili, I., Murtazashvili, J., & Salahodjaev, R. (2020b). Individualism and Governance of the Commons. *Public choice*, *184*(1), 175-195.

Cowan, W. N., Chang, T., Inglesi-Lotz, R., & Gupta, R. (2014). The nexus of electricity consumption, economic growth and CO2 emissions in the BRICS countries. *Energy Policy*, *66*, 359-368.

Durach, C. F., & Wiengarten, F. (2017). Environmental management: The impact of national and organisational long-term orientation on plants' environmental practices and performance efficacy. *Journal of Cleaner Production*, *167*, 749-758.

Efrat, K. (2014). The direct and indirect impact of culture on innovation. *Technovation*, *34*(1), 12-20.

Farzin, Y. H., & Bond, C. A. (2006). Democracy and environmental quality. *Journal of Development Economics*, *81*(1), 213-235.

Galor, O., & Özak, Ö. (2016). The agricultural origins of time preference. *American Economic Review*, *106*(10), 3064–3103.

Gorodnichenko, Y., & Roland, G. (2017). Culture, institutions, and the wealth of nations. *Review of Economics and Statistics*, *99*(3), 402-416.

Graafland, J. (2020). When does economic freedom promote well being? On the moderating role of long-term orientation. *Social Indicators Research*, *149*(1), 127-153.

Gul, M. C. (2013). Long-term orientation, perceived consumer effectiveness, and environmentally conscious consumer behavior: The case of Turkey. *International Journal of Marketing Studies*, *5*(5), 24.

Hofstede, G. (2011). Dimensionalizing cultures: The Hofstede model in context. *Online readings in psychology and culture*, 2(1), 2307-0919.

Hofstede, G., Hofstede, G.J., Minkov, M. (2010). *Cultures and organizations: Software of the mind*. Revised and expanded. McGraw-Hill, New York.

House, R. J., Hanges, P. J., Javidan, M., Dorfman, P. W., & Gupta, V. (2004). *Culture, leadership, and organizations. The Globe study of 62 societies*. Cambridge: Sage Publications.

Jang, Y., Ko, Y., & Kim, S. Y. (2016). Cultural correlates of national innovative capacity: a cross-national analysis of national culture and innovation rates. *Journal of Open Innovation: Technology, Market, and Complexity*, 2(4), 23.

Jo, A., & Carattini, S. (2021). Trust and CO2 emissions: Cooperation on a global scale. *Journal of Economic Behavior & Organization*, 190, 922-937.

Liu, X., Tu, R., Qiao, D., Niu, M., Li, R., Mao, Z., ... & Wang, C. (2020). Association between long-term exposure to ambient air pollution and obesity in a Chinese rural population: The Henan Rural Cohort Study. *Environmental Pollution*, 260, 114077.

Luechinger, S. (2010). Life satisfaction and transboundary air pollution. *Economics Letters*, 107(1), 4-6.

Lv, Z. (2017). The effect of democracy on CO2 emissions in emerging countries: does the level of income matter?. *Renewable and Sustainable Energy Reviews*, 72, 900-906.

Mallard, A. G., Lance, C. E., & Michalos, A. C. (1997). Culture as a moderator of overall life satisfaction–life facet satisfaction relationships. *Social Indicators Research*, 40(3), 259-284.

Masron, T. A., & Subramaniam, Y. (2019). Does poverty cause environmental degradation? Evidence from developing countries. *Journal of poverty*, 23(1), 44-64.

Matta, A. D., Gonçalves, F. L., & Bizarro, L. (2012). Delay discounting: Concepts and measures. *Psychology & Neuroscience*, 5(2), 135-146.

Mirzaei, M., & Bekri, M. (2017). Energy consumption and CO2 emissions in Iran, 2025. *Environmental research*, 154, 345-351.

Murtazashvili, I., Murtazashvili, J., & Salahodjaev, R. (2019). Trust and deforestation: A cross-country comparison. *Forest Policy and Economics*, 101, 111-119.

Ng, C. F. S., Stickley, A., Konishi, S., & Watanabe, C. (2016). Ambient air pollution and suicide in Tokyo, 2001–2011. *Journal of affective disorders*, 201, 194-202.

Park, S., & Lemaire, J. (2011). Culture Matters: Long-Term Orientation and the Demand for Life Insurance. *Asia-Pacific Journal of Risk and Insurance*, 5(2), 1-23.

Ruano-Ravina, A., Lema, L. V., Talavera, M. G., Gómez, M. G., Muñoz, S. G., Santiago-Pérez, M. I., ... & Pérez-Ríos, M. (2021). Lung cancer mortality attributable to residential radon exposure in Spain and its regions. *Environmental Research*, 111372.

Saboori, B., Sulaiman, J., & Mohd, S. (2012). Economic growth and CO2 emissions in Malaysia: a cointegration analysis of the environmental Kuznets curve. *Energy policy*, 51, 184-191.

Salahodjaev, R. (2018). Is there a link between cognitive abilities and environmental awareness? Cross-national evidence. *Environmental research*, 166, 86-90.

Shahbaz, M., Solarin, S. A., Sbia, R., & Bibi, S. (2015). Does energy intensity contribute to CO2 emissions? A trivariate analysis in selected African countries. *Ecological indicators*, 50, 215-224.

Shen, C. H., Fan, X., Huang, D., Zhu, H., & Wu, M. W. (2018). Financial development and economic growth: Do outliers matter? *Emerging Markets Finance and Trade*, *54*(13), 2925-2947.

Stern, D. I., Common, M. S., & Barbier, E. B. (1996). Economic growth and environmental degradation: the environmental Kuznets curve and sustainable development. *World development*, *24*(7), 1151-1160.

Wendling, Z. A., Emerson, J. W., de Sherbinin, A., Esty, D. C., et al., (2020). *2020 Environmental Performance Index.* New Haven, CT: Yale Center for Environmental Law & Policy. epi.yale.edu.

About Tashkent State University of Economics

Tashkent State University of Economics (TSUE) is the largest educational institution in Uzbekistan that prepares leaders. The university was founded on August 13, 1931 under the name of the Central Asian Institute of Finance and Economics. Since the establishment of the Tashkent State Economic University, more than 225 thousand specialists have been trained and in 2021 they celebrated the 90th anniversary with dignity.

Historical names of Tashkent State Economic University: Central Asian Financial and Economic Institute (1931-1936); Tashkent Institute of Finance and Economics (1936-1963); Tashkent Institute of National Economy (1963-1991); Tashkent State Economic University (since 1991).

Currently, the university has 5 faculties - Economics, Finance and Accounting, Corporate Governance, Digital Economy and International Tourism. Also, training activities have been established on the basis of an international joint educational program of double diplomas in cooperation with 9 International Universities.

More than 500 professors and teachers work at TSUE. Of these, 54 are doctors of sciences and 153 are candidates of sciences and teachers with a PhD degree.

Tashkent State University of Economics ranked in the 1000+ in the international rating "THE Impact Rankings 2021". It is ranked 3rd among local universities in the Webometrics ranking. It is included in the top 10 in the national rating of higher educational institutions of Uzbekistan.

About the Authors

Raufhon Salahodjaev (Editor/Author, Chapters 4, 8)
Raufhon Salahodjaev graduated from the Tashkent Institute of Finance in 2009 with a B.A. in Economics and Finance. He was the recipient of the Edmund S. Muskie Fellowship and studied at the State University of New York. He graduated from there with the degree of masters in Economics in 2011. He was a research intern at Cornell University in 2010.

Raufhon worked as Senior Research Fellow at Institute of Forecasting and Macroeconomic Research under the Cabinet of Ministers of the Republic of Uzbekistan from 2012 to 2018. He also worked as Associate lecturer at the Westminster International University in Tashkent. He received his PhD in economics from Tashkent Institute of Irrigation and Agricultural Mechanization Engineers based on the number of publications indexed in Web of Science and Scopus. His PhD advisor was professor O'ktam Pardayevich Umurzakov.

Raufhon Salahodjaev conducts academic and policy research on international economics, institutions, gender equality, sustainable development and human capital in both Eurasia and around the world. He has published more than 50 peer-reviewed journal articles in top journals across the social sciences. He also serves as associate professor at Tashkent State University of Economics and AKFA University (Uzbekistan).

Sharipov Kongratbay Avezimbetovich
Sharipov Kongratbay Avezimbetovich was born on March 24, 1963 in the Kungrad region of the Republic of Karakalpakstan into a family of employees. In 1986 he graduated from the Tashkent Institute of Irrigation and Agricultural Mechanization Engineers with a degree in Agricultural Mechanization.

From 1988 to 1992 he worked as a teacher-trainee, post-graduate student of the Moscow Institute of Agricultural Engineers named after V. P.

Goryachkin. In 1992 he successfully defended his candidate's thesis, and in 2005 he defended his doctoral dissertation in the specialty "Automobiles and tractors".

From 2003 to 2007 he was the general director of the Tashkent DAEWOO center; from 2007 to 2009 the general director of the Uzbek-Korean joint venture TOSHAFUS; and since 2009, the general director of GM Uzbekistan.

In 2009-2019, he worked first as a vice-rector and then as a rector of the Turin Polytechnic University in Tashkent.

In 2019, he served as First Deputy Minister of Higher and Secondary Special Education. He is currently the rector of the Tashkent State Economic University.

Doctor of Economics, Professor Sharipov K.A. during his scientific and pedagogical activity has prepared more than 20 textbooks and teaching guides and more than 10 monographs. Also, he is the scientific advisor of more than 10 candidates of sciences. He participated in many international and republican scientific conferences with scientific reports.

Eshov Mansur Pulatovich

Eshov Mansur Pulatovich graduated from the Faculty of Social Economic Regulation of the Tashkent State Economic University in 1998 and began his career in the Central Bank of the Republic of Uzbekistan. In 1999, he became the chief economist of the economic analysis and monitoring department of the Central Bank of the Republic of Uzbekistan.

From 1999 to 2002, he was a postgraduate student at the Tashkent State Economic University. From 2003 to 2004 he worked as an assistant at the Macroeconomics Department of the Tashkent State Economic University. From 2004 to 2006, working as a deputy dean of the Faculty of Economics and Statistics at the Tashkent State Economic University, he defended his Ph.D. thesis in macroeconomics.

From 2006 to 2007 he worked as an assistant to the rector of the Tashkent State Economic University.

In 2020, Eshov Mansur Pulatovich received a Doctor of Science (DSc) degree in areas 08.00.13 – "Finance, money circulation and credit" and 08.00.07 – "Management".

Since 2019, M. Eshov has been working as Vice-Rector for Academic Affairs of the Tashkent State University of Economics. He is the Chairman of the Scientific Council for awarding academic degrees in management.

He has published over 100 research papers, including, under the authorship of M. Eshov, 2 textbooks and 8 teaching guides 3 monographs and 35 articles were published in local and foreign journals and 28 articles and abstracts were presented at international conferences.

Abdurakhmanova Gulnora Kalandarovna

Abdurakhmanova Gulnora Kalandarovna was elected the head of the Department of Economics and Sociology of Labor at the Tashkent State Economic University in 2016. Since 2020, Gulnora Kalandarovna has been fruitfully working as vice-rector for research and innovation at the Tashkent State Economic University.

In 2017, at the Competition "The Best Teacher of Universities", she became the winner of the Republican stage in the nomination "Best Teacher-Researcher" in the field of economic education.

Gulnora Kalandarovna was awarded an honorary award for the 25th anniversary of the Constitution of the Republic of Uzbekistan and the 30th anniversary of the Independence of the Republic of Uzbekistan.

During her scientific and pedagogical activity, Abdurakhmanova Gulnora Kalandarovna conducts research in the field of labor economics, demography, human resource management. Today she is the chairman of the Scientific Council for the awarding of degrees in economics, works as an expert in the Scientific and Technical Council of the Ministry of Employment and Labor Relations and the Scientific and Technical Council of the Ministry of Innovative Development. Under her supervision, 3 researchers defended their PhD theses.

To date, she has published 100 scientific papers.

Zebo Kuldasheva

Zebo Kuldasheva is PhD scholar at Wuhan University, School of Economics. She obtained her master's degree from Central China Normal University in Business Administration with 3.5 GPA. During her studies abroad she attended various activities, conferences and was nominated with prestigious awards namely "Friendship Award", "Excellent International Student" and "Outstanding Extracurricular Award". Zebo conducts research in Environmental Economics, Energy Economics and Regional Economics. She published numerous papers in Web of Science and Scopus database including the highly ranked journals such as *Journal of Knowledge Economy and*

Economic Research as well as in Energy Economics journals. Currently working on the project "Energy poverty and industrial development".

Anastas Khachaturov
Anastas Khachaturov is an analyst at Ergo Analytics, Toshkent, Uzbekistan.

Akrom Ishnazarov
Akrom Ishnazarov is a scientist from Uzbekistan, a researcher in the field of econometric analysis of innovative approaches to economic growth and development of the country's economy. He graduated from the Tashkent State University of Economics (TSUE), and also studied at advanced training courses in the field of scientific research in countries such as the USA, Sweden, the Russian Federation. Author of over 50 articles in various national and international scientific journals. Teacher of the subject "Economic and mathematical methods and models" at TSUE.

Feruza Shamsiyeva
Feruza Shamsiyeva is a scientific researcher from Uzbekistan, conducting econometric research on the development of the country's exports, fruits and vegetables. She graduated from the Tashkent State University of Economics (TSUE) with a bachelor's and master's degree. She has published more than 25 articles in various national and international scientific journals. Teacher of the subject "Econometrics" at TSUE.

Askarova Feruza
Askarova Feruza is a scholar from Tashkent State University of Economics. She has graduated from Webster University with MBA degree. Prior to that she has graduated from TSUE with a degree in Business. She teaches foreign language classes at TSUE and conducts research in the areas of human capital, linguistic skills and quality of life. She has presented her research findings at a number of international conferences in social sciences.

Index

A

accumulation of human capital, 141

Africa, 5, 10, 15, 17, 22, 24, 32, 33, 38, 59, 69, 74, 83, 86, 148

Asia Pacific Economic Cooperation, 75, 87

B

Beck Depression Inventory, 123

C

capital flows, 72

capital inflow, 38, 43, 85

capital markets, 26, 42, 72

carbon emissions (CO_2 emissions), v, vii, 5, 7, 8, 14, 15, 16, 18, 34, 40, 43, 45, 48, 50, 51, 71, 75, 76, 77, 78, 79, 82, 83, 84, 85, 86, 87, 90, 91, 92, 93, 94, 95, 96, 97, 98, 99, 100, 111, 112, 113, 114, 115, 116, 117, 140, 148, 149

Central Asia, 35, 36, 40, 42, 48, 49, 151

China, vii, 6, 8, 18, 25, 37, 38, 39, 51, 52, 53, 57, 69, 70, 72, 74, 76, 86, 87, 94, 99, 100, 117, 135, 140

clean energy, 36, 48

climate change, 9, 36, 39, 72, 89, 90, 92, 96, 97, 111, 112, 116, 141, 142, 147, 148

climate change issues, 36, 39

CO2, vii, 5, 7, 8, 14, 15, 18, 40, 43, 45, 47, 48, 49, 50, 51, 71, 74, 75, 77, 79, 80, 82, 83, 84, 85, 86, 87, 89, 90, 91, 92, 93, 94, 95, 96, 97, 98, 99, 100, 101, 103, 106, 108, 109, 110, 111, 112, 113, 114, 115, 116, 117, 140, 148, 149

cointegration

cointegration, vii, 4, 6, 7, 8, 9, 11, 17, 21, 25, 27, 29, 30, 33, 35, 36, 44, 46, 49, 51, 52, 59, 71, 74, 75, 76, 80, 81, 84, 85, 86, 87, 89, 93, 94, 96, 100, 103, 104, 105, 108, 114, 115, 116, 117, 149

culture, v, 122, 134, 139, 140, 142, 146, 147, 148, 149

Czech Republic, 5, 25, 40, 76, 77, 98, 100

D

democracy, 26, 27, 29, 30, 70, 114, 140, 142, 143, 149

depression, v, 119, 120, 121, 122, 123, 124, 125, 126, 127, 128, 129, 130, 131, 132, 133, 134, 135, 136, 137

depressive symptoms, 121, 122, 123, 124, 129, 132, 133, 136

depth, 20, 26, 42

developed countries, 1, 32, 58, 59, 69, 70

developed nations, 71

developing countries, vii, 37, 52, 91, 97, 98, 112, 114, 149

developing economies, 38, 97

development, v, vii, 1, 3, 4, 6, 8, 9, 14, 15, 16, 17, 18, 19, 20, 21, 22, 24, 25, 26, 27, 28, 29, 30, 31, 32, 33, 34, 35, 36, 38, 39, 40, 41, 42, 43, 45, 46, 47, 48, 49, 50, 51, 52, 53, 57, 59, 61, 69, 70, 72, 74, 84, 87, 89, 90, 91, 93, 94, 95, 96, 99, 100, 102, 110, 111, 112, 113, 114, 115, 116, 117, 120, 121, 126, 132, 135, 136, 141, 148, 150, 155